# Collateral Language

A User's Guide to America's New War

**Edited by John Collins and Ross Glover**

 New York University Press • New York and London

**NEW YORK UNIVERSITY PRESS**
New York and London

© 2002 by New York University Press
All rights reserved

Library of Congress Cataloging-in-Publication Data
Collateral language : a user's guide to America's new war /
[edited by] John Colins, Ross Glover.
p. cm.
Includes bibliographical references and index.
ISBN 0–8147–1627–X (cloth : alk. paper) —
ISBN 0–8147–1628–8 (pbk. : alk. paper)
1. War on Terrorism, 2001–   2. Rhetoric—Political
aspects—United States.   I. Collins, John.   II. Glover, Ross.
HV6432 .C64 2002
973.931—dc21          2002007063

New York University Press books are printed on acid-free paper,
and their binding materials are chosen for strength and durability.

Manufactured in the United States of America
10 9 8 7 6 5 4 3 2

# Collateral Language

# Contents

# Acknowledgments

In putting this book together, we benefited from the reading, the encouragement, and the logistical assistance of numerous individuals. First, we want to express our deep appreciation to the contributors, who produced their chapters and artwork under intense time pressure. Without their willingness to set aside other personal and professional commitments in the face of extraordinary circumstances, we could not have completed the book in such a timely fashion.

We are also grateful to the many St. Lawrence University students who agreed to read parts of the book, providing us with valuable feedback on the project, and to our faculty colleagues at St. Lawrence who encouraged us to pursue the project in the first place, and particularly the Global Studies Department.

Given that the book emerged in the immediate aftermath of September 11, the work gathered here is inevitably a product of that time. The final months of 2001 saw not only an upsurge in the predictable, often uncritical rhetoric of patriotism and militarism, but also a tremendous number of articles written by courageous men and women who dared to ask questions, to resist the manufactured inevitability of war, and to place the events of September 11 in a broader political context. As authors, we are profoundly indebted to these critical voices, some of whom—Arundhati Roy, Robert Fisk, Edward Said, and others—are referenced in the book.

Stephen Magro and the staff at NYU Press were extremely helpful and easy to work with from the beginning of the project. Thanks to Zone 4 for permission to use several of the images that separate the chapters. Finally, a special thanks goes to Stephen Pfohl, who got the ball rolling by helping us with initial contacts.

# Introduction

JOHN COLLINS AND ROSS GLOVER

Language is a terrorist organization, and we stand united against terrorism. This book is a collection of essays written to expose the tyranny of political rhetoric used to justify "America's New War." From Buchenwald to Rwanda, from Wounded Knee to Watts, from the gulags of Stalinist Russia to the massacres of Sabra and Shatila, from San Salvador to Srebernica, the killing fields of the modern world respect no national boundaries. All these places are, in a sense, the same place, where the practices of war destroy the dream of human rights. In October 2001, the United States marshaled all its resources and began bombing one of those places, Afghanistan, shamefully sending one of the poorest countries in the world back onto the list of global war zones. U.S. officials, like their counterparts in decades past, attempted to generate public support for their actions by appealing to ideas as powerful as they are abstract: freedom, civilization, terrorism, evil. This language needs interrogation wherever it is found. The essays in this book explore the use of such language by American political leaders and mainstream media outlets in the wake of the September 11th attacks.

We entitle this book *Collateral Language* to illustrate that while language always shapes our lives, the effects of language during war are unique. Just as "collateral damage" describes military damage in addition to the intended targets, "collateral language" refers to the language war as a practice adds to our ongoing lexicon as well as to the additional meaning certain terms acquire during wartime. We call language a terrorist organization to illustrate the real effects of language on citizens, especially in times of war. Language, like terrorism, targets civilians and generates fear in order to effect political change. When our political leaders and our media outlets use terms like Anthrax, terrorist threat, madmen, and biological weapons, a specific type of fearfulness emerges, both intentionally and unintentionally. We are all targets for this type of language, and we are all affected by it as well. Regardless of the truth of the words, collateral language produces effects beyond its meaning. The title *Collateral Language* and the reference to language as a terrorist organization highlight these effects.

Numerous terms and phrases emerge during war to describe, justify, and explain a nation's actions to the people of that nation. The U.S. political-military lexicon utilizes terms in particular ways to produce desired responses from its citizens. Most of these terms are familiar to us, and we often seem to respond to them as if they carry meaningful and specific messages. However, interrogating the history and development of such terms often leads to an awareness that their meanings change and their effects can kill. The use of specific kinds of language for political purposes exists within a long historical lineage of human development, and in order to understand any political system, we must understand the meaning created by that system. Rather than blindly accepting the meaning, usage, and truth of political leaders and news stories, we have an obligation, as citizens of a democratic state, to question, critique, and understand the language given to us by those who claim to represent our interests. With this in mind, we have developed five broad ways of understanding the impact of language on us as citizens: consent, perception, real effects, history, and possibility. Each essay in this collection reflects on one or more of these; taken together, they offer a more sophisticated and interesting way to hear the rhetoric distributed by the mainstream media and our political leaders.

## Manufacturing Consent

A central project of any political rhetoric is to develop support from the people. The most stark example of this process in the twentieth century was Hitler's Germany. Using the language of unification distributed through sophisticated propaganda techniques, Hitler managed to turn many of his nation's people into racist murderers. The lesson many suggest we must learn, and often learn again, is that even the most "civilized" people are potential killers, if they are convinced of the "rightness" or "necessity" of their actions. This period teaches us another important lesson: if the state knows how to use the correct language, it can convince its people to commit the most atrocious acts. The twentieth century has seen the United States develop a sophisticated set of linguistic tools (some might say weapons) to manufacture broad-based consent and support for both domestic and foreign policies. These tools are not perfect, as protests against the Vietnam War exemplify. However, linguistic tools are continually modified, especially in the case of their failure, and U.S. political strategists learned much from Vietnam. This is exactly why the news media has been refused access to U.S. actions in Panama, Iraq, and Afghanistan in recent years. The more control the state has over the language a population hears and the images it sees, the easier it is to develop "democratic" consent.

The use of vague terms for creating the consent of the U.S. population is one strategy employed by political leaders. Many of the essays in *Collateral Language* highlight this reality. Terms such as freedom, justice, terrorism, and evil offer excellent examples of how language can be utilized to produce consent. We all want freedom and justice and we all oppose evil and terrorism, but we rarely question the meaning of these terms; we believe we know what they mean until we attempt to define them. Thus a politician employing this type of language can justify a variety of different actions with impunity. "In order to protect our freedom, we must overthrow the evil government of [insert country]." Criticizing this type of statement is difficult at best because most people want freedom and only a few actively support evil. This simple example demonstrates the way in which a complex, geopolitical decision gets the support of many without the need for understanding the specific meaning of anything.

## What You Hear Is What You See

More broadly than simple consent, language, as something particularly human, shapes how we see the world in general. From knowing the basic difference between an apple and a hand grenade to knowing which is better to have in a specific situation, language is imperative. While we do not always realize it, language acts as a determinate factor in the formation of our perceptions of the world. For example, one person might look at an SUV and think "what an excellent automobile," while another person might look at that same vehicle and think "what a gas-guzzling detriment to the environment." Language shapes each of these responses. Had the second person not heard about global warming, $CO_2$ emissions, and the gas mileage an SUV gets, he or she probably would not have had such a negative response. However, given knowledge of these things, the SUV may literally not look like such a nice vehicle. This type of linguistic understanding can refer to anything in our lives, but for the purposes of this book, it seems most important to focus on the political arena. To seriously understand political rhetoric, a recognition that what we hear does significantly affect the way we see the world and how we see specific people in that world is in order.

The United States has a long history of racial segregation and discrimination, and that history illustrates how language determines our perceptions. In broad strokes, we might imagine how white people spoke about people with dark skin during the early part of U.S. history. Dark-skinned people were often referred to as primitive or as animals. This language justified the brutal enslavement and exploitation of those people. In the twenty-first century race continues to be an issue, but the perceptions of people with dark skin have changed significantly. Rather than being characterized by language that would permit slavery, African American people are now often connected, through language, with crime, poverty, laziness, and drugs. This creates specific types of racial perceptions that fail to give an accurate presentation of race, but are also very different from those perceptions during slavery. Seeing a group of black men walking down the streets of a major city might produce very different feelings for some individuals than seeing a group of white men. The two groups might be equally likely to be violent or not, but in many cases, the group of black men will be perceived as more dangerous—language creates our perceptions.

This understanding of language becomes especially important when thinking through the developments since September 11, 2001. Since that time, a perceptual system emerged linking up any person who appeared "as if" they were Middle Eastern. The immediate increase in racially motivated crimes after the bombings demonstrates the significance of these perceptions. We begin as a country to perceive danger in people based on skin color, or on the association of certain types of bodily features with threats such as Anthrax (see "Anthrax"). By early November, the

U.S. government had arrested over a thousand people, virtually all of whom were either Arab or Muslim, in most cases without charge. This was the most significant detention of a racial group since the internment of Japanese Americans during World War II. While these detentions may seem justified to some, it is important to remember that after the Oklahoma City bombings, the government did not arrest anyone whose name sounded Irish except Timothy McVeigh. Nor did we come to see all white people, Christians, or former Marines as suspected terrorists after these bombings. With this in mind, the impact of language on perception becomes clear. Because the Middle Easterner has been linked through language with terrorism, it is easy to see all people who resemble someone from that region of the world as possible terrorists. This aspect of language helps governments manufacture consent for discrimination against particular groups of people.

## The Real Effects of Language

As any university student knows, theories about the "social construction" and social effects of language have become a common feature of academic scholarship. Conservative critics often argue that those who use these theories of language (e.g., deconstruction) are "just" talking about language, as opposed to talking about the "real world." The essays in this book, by contrast, begin from the premise that language matters in the most concrete, immediate way possible: its use, by political and military leaders, leads directly to violence in the form of war, mass murder (including genocide), the physical destruction of human communities, and the devastation of the natural environment. Indeed, if the world ever witnesses a nuclear holocaust, it will probably be because leaders in more than one country have succeeded in convincing their people, through the use of political language, that the use of nuclear weapons and, if necessary, the destruction of the earth itself, is justifiable. From our perspective, then, every act of political violence—from the horrors perpetrated against Native Americans to the murder of political dissidents in the Soviet Union to the destruction of the World Trade Center, and now the bombing of Afghanistan—is intimately linked with the use of language.

Partly what we are talking about here, of course, are the processes of "manufacturing consent" and shaping people's perception of the world around them; people are more likely to support acts of violence committed in their name if the recipients of the violence have been defined as "terrorists," or if the violence is presented as a defense of "freedom." Media analysts such as Noam Chomsky have written eloquently about the corrosive effects that this kind of process has on the political culture of supposedly democratic societies. At the risk of stating the obvious, however, the most fundamental effects of violence are those that are visited upon the objects of violence; the language that shapes public opinion is the same language that burns villages, besieges entire populations, kills and maims human bodies, and leaves the ground scarred with bomb craters and littered with land mines. As George Orwell so famously illustrated in his work, acts of violence can easily be made more palatable through the use of euphemisms such as "pacification" or, to use an example discussed in this book, "targets." It is important to point out, however, that the need for such language derives from the simple fact that the violence itself is abhorrent. Were it not for the abstract language of "vital interests" and "surgical strikes" and the flattering language of "civilization" and "just" wars, we would be less likely to avert our mental gaze from the physical effects of violence.

The link between language and violence works in at least two ways which combine to create an endless cycle of justification.

First, language helps to create a climate in which the need for military action appears to be self-evident. Almost immediately after September 11, supposedly "objective" journalists were echoing politicians and pundits by saying, "The United States has no choice but to respond," thereby giving the subsequent war an aura of inevitability. Administration officials and sympathetic commentators fueled the same process with similar remarks: "We must respond forcefully to terrorism," or "If we do nothing, we will encourage more terrorism." By the time the U.S. military began raining bombs down on Afghanistan in early October, the use of language had already prepared the groundwork, and little public opposition was heard. In terms of media coverage, the new war has made the highly managed Gulf War of 1991 look like an unrestricted festival of investigative reporting. Yet even in such a controlled information environment, the existence of violence has the potential to generate revulsion on the part of the reading and viewing public, and this is where language plays a second, related role.

The military language that is so widely repeated in the media softens the visceral impact of the violence on ordinary citizens. To speak of "collateral damage" is a far cry from acknowledging the blown-off limbs, the punctured eardrums, the shrapnel wounds, and the psychological horror that are caused by heavy bombardment; even speaking of "civilian casualties" deflects attention from the real effects of the bombs. Such euphemisms ("aerial sorties," "Taliban positions," "smart bombs") work in two directions, both making the already committed violence more palatable and softening up the public so that future military actions will seem more like video games and less like what they are—acts of violence that result in death, injury, and destruction.

## Language and History

Words have histories. This is an element of language that animates all the essays in this collection. Listening to the pronouncements of those who hold power in the United States, of course, one would be tempted to conclude that this is not the case. When a word like "evil" is invoked, for example, it is almost as if the word has simply dropped from the sky with a meaning that is as universally clear as it is unchanging. A historical view would show that the Americans' belief that their government is incapable of committing acts of "evil" has much to do with the fact that Americans have been hearing, throughout their lives, about the "evil" that resides in "other" places (the Soviet Union, Cuba, Iraq). This is what makes it possible for George W. Bush (or any other prominent public official) to speak of "evildoers" and to have his words be both understood and unchallenged. People who hijack airplanes and kill civilians are evil; what could be clearer? Step outside the circle of U.S. public debate, however, and you discover little consensus around Bush's use of this term. Supporters of Osama bin Laden clearly see the September 11 attacks as the very antithesis of evil and may therefore use other words ("heroic," "justified") to describe the attacks; others in the Middle East may condemn the attacks but insist that they were simply misguided, not evil. Others around the world may have memories of violent American actions in the past, memories that cause them to look with some skepticism on current U.S. attempts to define "evil" for everyone.

Words, then, have no inherent meanings; instead, they have to be made to mean something. Processes of meaning-making don't happen overnight; rather, they happen historically, through repeated, often calculated, and generally selective usage. Over a long period of time, the efforts of the political, economic, and media elite to "get our consent" has the effect of making certain meanings seem "natural" and reducing our ability to see through those meanings, or beyond them. Even though meanings can never be entirely fixed—for, as we will see in the following section, there is always room for other possibilities—they can be controlled and used to generate significant degrees of public consensus. Nowhere is this clearer than during the initial stages of wars and other major military interventions, when words like "justice" and "freedom" fill the air and the approval ratings of presidents skyrocket along with the stock prices of arms manufacturers.

When we look at words in this way, it is clear that unearthing the histories of words—that is, identifying and naming the social forces that have combined to fix the meaning of particular words—can be an act of intellectual and political resistance. The fact that a group of conservative American theologians got together in the late nineteenth century to define the "fundamentals" of the Christian faith, and that the notion of "fundamentals" was later popularized by two brothers whose wealth came from oil (see "Fundamentalism"), may seem a mildly interesting but ultimately marginal historical detail; yet in the current context, knowledge of this history can help us generate a critical perspective on how the notion of "Islamic fundamentalism" is being used to create support for war. Similarly, the very idea of declaring a "war on terrorism" may seem obvious and unproblematic—until we consider that this war bears an interesting resemblance to the "war on drugs" and even the "war on poverty" of the 1960s (see "The War on ———"). In short, all the essays contained here suggest that the importance of words lies not in the words themselves, but rather in the way they are used, by whom, and to what effect. More specifically, these essays demonstrate that one of the best ways to understand the meaning of "collateral language" is to connect the present use of terms with what is often a long historical development.

## The Possibility of Language

While the history of language always represents an important component of the way that language affects us, we want to make absolutely clear that a central feature of language is change. The power of language to manufacture consent resides in its ability to be adapted to various situations in different time periods. This same strength also leads to its ability to work against the political development of consent. One of the most striking things in the aftermath of the WTC attacks was the almost complete elimination of dissenting voices, and the vicious criticisms leveled at those who offered dissenting voices to the Bush Administration, or even to the language used to discuss the events. Bill Maher, for example, lost his contract for the television show *Politically Incorrect* (the name itself demands it state the unpopular opinion) because he suggested that it was more cowardly to launch missiles from a thousand miles away than to fly a plane into a building (see "Cowardice"), and Congresswoman Barbara Lee (D-California) was seriously criticized for casting the lone vote against giving George W. Bush absolute discretion in the military response to terrorism (see "Unity"). In fact, *Collateral Language* as a project emerged as a response to the silencing of critical voices.

Language need not conform to any one political agenda, but when used by the state, it can seem to do so. This book demonstrates how language helps manufacture consent and demonstrates that language, sometimes the same language, creates the possibility of dissent. Neither the state, the media, political pundits, nor religious leaders own the words they use to sway our belief. In this sense, speech is always free, at least to the degree that we make it such. We make language mean specific things, and if we so choose, we can make words mean what we feel they should mean, rather than what a talking head tries to make them mean. Every essay in this collection attempts, in one way or another, to address this reality. We are not interested in creating a new language, but in permitting the language given us in times of war to mean something else. We do, however, believe that some terms have more possibility than others. Some terms of war seem to us in need of replacement. Specifically, words used to minimize the impact of war such as targets, collateral damage, civilization, barbarism, war on, and terrorism need to be replaced by terms more likely to represent reality. For example, "collateral damage" could be replaced by "excessive destruction." Any time a term minimizes the real destructive impact of our actions or minimizes the humanity of large groups of people, we believe it needs serious interrogation and possible reformation.

Not all terms used during wartime, however, need to be discarded. A host of terms in *Collateral Language* require a full recognition of their possibilities. Words such as freedom, justice, and unity represent the possibility to truly transform our most destructive tendencies. Instead of allowing those words to blind us into consent, we can demand their legitimate use. Rather than hearing freedom and justice as calls to war, we can use these terms ourselves to understand how war may compromise those very concepts. Rather than using unity as a word to pit one group against another, the term could come to mean connecting with others to create a global democracy. We might begin, then, imagining a world in which everyone participates in the decision-making process. Such a world might question using the word peace as a justification for war. It might recognize that sustained military control of any area in the world reduces freedom. Such a world resides, to a large degree, in the possibility of language; in our ability to make words mean something different; in our commitment to take action in the face of consent; and in our willingness to demand that the possibilities of language be developed. *Collateral Language* takes a step in this direction, and as editors, we hope you find in these pages new ways to hear the world around you and the possibility to make that world a more just, free, and humane place.

### SUGGESTIONS FOR FURTHER READING

Chomsky, Noam, and Edward Herman. *Manufacturing Consent: The Political Economy of the Mass Media.* New York: Pantheon Books, 1988.

Herman, Edward S. *Beyond Hypocrisy: Decoding the News in an Age of Propaganda.* Boston: South End Press, 1992.

Lakoff, George. "Metaphors of Terror." September 16, 2001 (www.press.uchicago.edu/News/911lakoff.html).

Williams, Raymond. *Keywords: A Vocabulary of Culture and Society.* Rev. ed. New York: Oxford University Press, 1985.

Zone 4, *Fear and Desire. Reprinted with the permission of Zone 4.*

# 1. Anthrax

R. Danielle Egan

This story, my story of Anthrax and what Anthrax symbolically represents in our broader culture, starts with me in my pajamas. Fuzzy brained and in the process of waking up, clutching my coffee as I move from the kitchen and into the living room, I grab the remote control and turn on CNN. A nice white woman with a southern accent is being interviewed: "So, tell us about your cause," the male reporter from CNN says. During the delay, while his words travel to her in Lafayette, Tennessee, from Atlanta, the camera pans to the name of the street on which she is standing—Anthrax Street. The blonde woman with the soothing accent goes on to talk about her disgust with the name of the street on which she lives and how "people stand back when they read the name of [her] street on [her] checks." During her narrative the reporter on the split screen nods empathetically because who in America would want to live on Anthrax Street? The reporter asks, "So what are you planning?" The woman explains that she is passing around a petition to her neighbors to change the name of her street. "Have any of your neighbors given you suggestions on what they would like to see the name of the street changed to?" "Yes," she replies, and goes on to list names like "America," "Freedom," and "U.S.A." The reporter wishes the woman good luck with her cause, to which she says "Thank you," and the next story starts.

When next year's map of Lafayette, Tennessee, is published, will there will be an Anthrax Street, or will Anthrax become America, Freedom, or U.S.A. Street? Even if the name is changed you can be sure that Anthrax Street will be a ghostly presence that haunts the map, a reminder of the cultural panic when names of streets caused people to stand back when they read it on checks and when parents discussed whether there should be Halloween due to the possibility of Anthrax-tainted candy given to children in their trick or treat bags. Meanwhile, what will happen to the maps with Anthrax Street on them? Will they become collector's items selling on Ebay with "Operation Enduring Freedom" trading cards?

This story of a blonde woman in a panic over the name of her street represents a fear of infestation. Is she possibly guilty of infection by association due to the street on which she lives? Just to be safe, she distances herself as far as possible from it, changing her street name from a dis-ease, to something strong and seemingly pure like America or Freedom. To live on Anthrax Street is to be associated with terrorism, with "weapons of mass destruction," and finally with terrorists.[1] After my cup of coffee, my mind cleared, and I sat in awe as I thought about how Anthrax has come to symbolically represent the Middle Eastern "terrorist" body, and how this bacterium serves as proof of the fragility of our own national, capitalist, and cultural border. Moreover, Anthrax and our "internal war" against it seek to shore up these boundaries to protect the social body from invasion by an almost invisible plague in our midst.

As in other wartime conflicts, America at this point in time metaphorically takes on the quality of a body that is under attack from invasion and needs to be protected from the "other" who can infect the "life blood" or "livelihood" of a nation.[2] Since

9/11, the metaphor of the social body that represents America comes to operate even more powerfully when the body is seemingly under attack from a biological weapon such as Anthrax. Anthrax, like other dis-eases that have caused cultural panics, such as HIV/AIDS, serves as a discourse which merges a biological disease with a population which also causes social dis-ease, the Middle Eastern body for Anthrax and the body of the homosexual male for HIV/AIDS.

In the early 1980s the discourse of HIV/AIDS created a social panic that functioned to identify HIV exclusively with male homosexuals. In so doing, this discourse stigmatized all gay men as potential dis-ease carriers. A homophobic synecdochic doubling occurred wherein one gay man came to represent all gay men as diseased, and HIV in one man came to represent the fantasy that all gay men were diseased.[3] Seropositivity was seen as emblematic of gay sexuality. In this homophobic discourse, a panic ensued over the potential that the pure heterobody was in danger from gay men who were getting what they deserved due to their "deviant lifestyle." This discourse perpetuated homophobic responses that ranged from lack of research money to right-wing fundamental Christian ministers offering solutions such as shipping those with HIV to sparsely populated areas to insure the purity of the heterobody.[4]

However, unlike the homophobia which circulated around HIV/AIDS in the early 1980s where gay men were prefigured as the carriers of the plague that could infest the "pure" heterosexual body, Anthrax functions somewhat differently because the afflicted are viewed as pure, and the mysterious senders who are unafflicted are viewed as demonic and evil, not only infecting the individual body, but infecting the immune system of the social body as well. With the closing of post offices, the Congress, and the Supreme Court, the social body faces a bacterium that could cripple institutional sites which had not been closed since their inception. Through the discourse of Anthrax, the United States represents a social body whose immune system is under attack—by those infected not with a biological disease but with a political and religious one instead. Anthrax gets merged with the bodies of those from the Middle East so that they represent one and the same thing. It is this synthesis which underlies the cultural panic sweeping the United States.[5]

A function of the discourse of Anthrax and its production of panic is the construction of Anthrax as a weapon of mass destruction. This creates both the illusion and the panic necessary for its cultural acceptability. Anthrax as weapon of mass destruction extends this discourse to its ultimate limit, meaning that if Anthrax is a weapon of mass destruction, then any and all governmental intervention is not only valid but also absolutely necessary for national safety. This, in effect, makes the continual bombing of Afghanistan seem necessary and the next potential target, Iraq, prudent. We are being bombarded, we are under attack, the body America is in danger by a weapon of mass destruction; therefore, we must strengthen our immune system—we must fight back. We must protect ourselves by any means necessary. The use of the term "weapon of mass destruction" in the discourse of Anthrax is the ultimate illusion, the ultimate way of producing a cultural panic and blindness to the massive contradiction between Anthrax, which has at this time killed four people, and the repeated dropping of ten-ton bombs on Afghanistan. The contradiction in logic is so obvious, but so obscured. How can a bacterium that a simple sixty-day course of the antibiotic Cipro can cure be viewed as more threatening than the continual air raids in Afghanistan? Or the "daisy cutter" bombs that incinerate a one-square-mile area?

The United States has repeatedly used weapons of mass destruction, whether one thinks of the napalm used in Vietnam, the atomic weapons dropped on Japan, or the not-so-"smart" bombs in Iraq which killed thousands of innocent Iraqi civilians—or the embargo which has been estimated to have cost close to a million children their lives in Iraq. Or, if we go back further in history, the smallpox-infested blankets sent to Native Americans by the U.S. government, an action that cost thousands of lives. Weapons of mass destruction are defined as those that can kill large numbers of people through nuclear, biological, or chemical means. I would argue that there is a need to recognize that conventional weapons such as daisy cutters, smart bombs, and cluster bombs with their ability to take large numbers of lives, particularly in repeated air raids, are weapons of mass destruction. To do so would force the United States to explore its own mass destruction in other countries, destruction that has been ideologically ignored under the guise of "protection of U.S. interests." Our discursively produced panic has effectively wiped out our cultural understanding of past and present U.S. atrocities.

An article on Anthrax from my local newspaper declared, "in the longer run, both possibilities [Anthrax contamination through the mail attacking political institutions as well as spreading beyond its intended targets] raise the question of whether the U.S. mail stream as a whole may at some point have to be deemed potentially deadly."[6] CNN and other mainstream news organizations report that those in the public eye, from members of Congress to soap opera stars, are now fearful of their mail. People are encouraged to send their favorite stars e-mails as opposed to letters through the mail. However, no official statement has yet been released from Hollywood. Oprah Winfrey has a panic-ridden audience being counseled by Dr. Phil, who tells them that their fear is unnecessary and that they are the only ones holding themselves hostage. All precautions must be taken and are being taken, we are told by Ari Flescher, and we must stay calm while Anthrax spores are found in post offices in New Jersey, New York, Florida, and Washington, D.C. The Postmaster

General states that there are no guarantees of complete mail safety. Moreover, Vice President Dick Cheney reports that he is suspicious that the attack of September 11 and the attacks of Anthrax are linked.

When viewing the media coverage, it seems as if our Congress, president, Supreme Court Justices, and news anchors are under attack, yet suspiciously the "targets" of these attacks are continuously unscathed, whether we are talking about Senator Daschle or Tom Brokaw. Anthrax seems only to touch those who serve such powerful figures; like the food tasters who protected the monarch from potential poisoning, it is interns, secretaries, post office workers, or assistants—the least protected—who should be considered at risk. It is no wonder that residents of Ewing, New Jersey, met to allay their fears of Anthrax and are subsequently washing their mailboxes with a bleach and water solution, which should kill any dangerous bacteria. These stories underscore the need for panic and support the belief that our social body is presently under attack. However, like many wars it is usually those who reside in nonpowerful positions who are most affected (see "War on _____").

The individually infected body has been enlarged to become the social body so that the infected postal worker or the exposed NBC employee becomes the infected or exposed body of America. Whether it is cutaneous or inhaled Anthrax, the discourse underscores that we are in danger, that terrorism has transgressed the internal lines of the social body. The Anthrax-laden letters are available for all to see at CNN.com, providing a type of visible evidence and justification for the panic presently sweeping the United States. Specular proof is a currency in our culture. We need to see it to believe it, so to speak. Next to the letters that circulate on television and in cyberspace, we can see microscopic images of the Anthrax bacterium and associate those images as the cause of our panic and potential infection. The visual image perpetuates both the discourse of Anthrax and the panic that accompanies it, because the visual acts as a form of truth and proof that our social body is under attack and that the body America is in a seemingly precarious and vulnerable state. Moreover, it provides truth and justification for our need to fight back. The microscopic pictures of Anthrax, like "ground zero," provide scopic justification for our war and governmental policies, both domestic and international, in this war.

Culturally, we have come to deal with this transgression of the social body by equating the Anthrax spore with the Middle Eastern body. Moreover, this discourse serves to make the Middle Eastern body synonymous with the Islamic, Arab, and other "brown bodies" which all come to equal "terrorist." Anthrax is the Middle Eastern Other and, like the environmental sweeps that go on in various buildings across the country, so too under our antiterrorism legislation are the largest sweeps of bodies of color—namely, Middle Eastern bodies, being detained in numbers we have not seen since the Japanese internment camps of World War II. The Islamic body is a potential infection that must be contained before it spreads, before it is ingested and kills the body America. The discourse of Anthrax couples racist and xenophobic fears of the "other" and their seeming ability to gestate among us.

These fears increase an insidious form of U.S. state power which many have accepted for their own good and protection, seeking to rid the social body of its infection. Like the side effects associated with an antibiotic, we must be willing to deal with the side effects of "homeland security"—it will, after all, "make us feel better." Like the cancer patient who undergoes radiation treatments that make him or her sicker in the hope of getting better, we accept the abolishment of our civil rights in the hope of making the body America better in the long run. This is evidenced in polls on CNN that state that American citizens are willing to forgo certain rights and suffer inconveniences in order to rid our country of terrorism.

Terrorist cells become Anthrax colonies, and in this coupling a form of synthesis occurs due to the visual interchanging of terrorist = Middle Eastern. Like the discourse of HIV/AIDS, the discourse of Anthrax also produces a form of synecdochic doubling. All Middle Eastern bodies come to be associated in the United States with terrorism (as evidenced in the suspect sweeps of Middle Eastern people) and through the discourse of Anthrax, all terrorists, and thus Middle Eastern bodies, become associated with Anthrax. The three become one, producing a sensibility and justification for the panic and fear perpetuated by the discourse of Anthrax and the tactics necessary to combat the problem. As such, people who fit a particular corporeal image are guilty prior to ever doing anything wrong.

The racialization of visual difference between white and non-white produces a system wherein anyone of Arab descent is automatically registered as guilty. The visual field of the police officer, the INS officer, military guard, or worried citizen is saturated by a discourse which constructs the Middle Eastern body as infectious; the effect of the process serves to replace the category of "suspect" with "infectious." The Middle Eastern body, in other words, is suspected and thus infecting long before an action ever takes place. Like the spore exposure that leads to Anthrax, the Middle Eastern or Islamic body is a form of exposure that could lead to cultural infection.

Through this racist coupling of Anthrax with the Islamic or Middle Eastern body, the discourse of Anthrax serves another purpose, as a justification for civil rights violations in our homeland security tactics and the continued bombing of Afghanistan or potentially other countries that are "against us" and therefore, "terrorists." Although the official governmental discourse suggests that we stay calm and that we have nothing to worry about, the cultural panic is to the government's advantage as it justifies our "war" on two fronts, in the United States and in Afghanistan.

This panic blinds the population by warping their perceptions through fear. Attorney General John Ashcroft stated that terrorist cells still exist and we need to root them out; he further stated that terrorists "are poisoning our communities with Anthrax." The use of "terrorist cells" by the government invokes another disease—cancer. Like the metastatic rogue cell in the body, the terrorist cell is pathological and needs cutting out before its pathology spreads to the larger social body. This discourse perpetuates the perception that the spore/terrorists are everywhere, thereby justifying the rounding up of nine hundred and ninety "suspects" since 9/11. These roundups or sweeps are viewed as "necessary" in our fight against "evil." Yet out of the nine hundred and ninety detainees only ten have any known connection with 9/11, and a fifty-five-year old man detained by the Department of Immigration and Naturalization Services (INS) has died "mysteriously" in prison. This alone is sufficient for a cultural panic surrounding the erosion of our civil rights; however, our Anthrax panic creates a discourse that hides abuse of power and lack of due process, and, in effect, creates an ideology making these sweeps a necessary result of our internal war to protect the immune system of body America. America will never be the same, they say; however, if we examine the history of U.S. foreign policy and FBI tactics domestically we see the ghost of violations past rearing its ugly head, similitude in its worst form.

The formation of the discourse on bioterrorism is new in that it is being filtered through the media and government as a "new type of warfare," one that is not people strapping on bombs, but rather insidiously infecting us while the perpetrators go unscathed. It is, however, in the effects of this discourse that we see the past repeating itself. We only need to scratch the surface to see the ways in which the United States has violated human rights in the name of protecting its hegemonic interests. Whether it is the training of dictators of Central and South America at the School of the Americas in Georgia who under the discourse of capitalism and democracy systematically kill leftists and the poor who challenge the hegemony of U.S. domination; or the FBI killing Black Panthers in their beds to protect the white populations from the potential violence of black nationalism; or the rounding up of socialists during the "red scare"; or the U.S. military using biological weapons in previous conflicts—the United States abuses power and constrains dissent at every turn.

This illuminates how the United States creates discursive smoke screens to conduct horrific violence against those who grate against the dominant ideologies of the state and its interests. The most effective way to do this is to create a discourse that perpetuates panic and makes the population feel there is no other choice. This is the discourse of Anthrax. Racism and xenophobia make the discourse all the more powerful. Precisely because the Middle Eastern body is nonwhite, civil rights violations become easier and culturally palatable. After the Oklahoma City bombing it would have been impossible to categorize the white terrorists as anything other than "a few bad extremists," otherwise whiteness itself would have come under suspicion.

Currently, training courses are being advertised on-line which offer to train officers, guards, military, and other law enforcers to combat bioterrorism. Ironically, these training sessions are in Georgia—the site of the School of the Americas discussed above—showing the ghostly presence of this "new" form of counterterrorism. Although its syllabi are not available to the public, I wonder what strategies it employs, how much more in the name of homeland security will we give up, how many more of our rights and the rights of others we will hand over. Due to the racialized status of the terrorists, sweeps of Middle Eastern "others" are justified and the distinction between these "others" and Anthrax collapses. The discourse of Anthrax, the fear it produces, and its underlying use of xenophobia are countered by homeland security as a discursive placebo effect. A placebo effect takes place when a patient thinks he or she is being given medication, when in fact the medication is nothing but sugar pills. Placebos produce biological results without utilizing a biological agent. Psychosomatically the placebo generates for the patient a feeling of cure—that everything will be okay. The discourse of homeland security functions similarly. It is a placebo that produces a type of cultural psychosomatic cure wherein people feel better. Safety is the feeling produced; however, our sickness, namely the strategies that the United States is undertaking, harms the social body far more than Anthrax ever could. This discursive placebo functions to keep the dangers of civil rights violations internally hazy at best and justifies the bombing of Afghanistan as well as other Middle Eastern countries.

The placebo effect produced by the language of homeland security creates a psychosomatic calm, making the racism and xenophobia in the Anthrax discourse almost invisible. However, if we listen closely, we can hear a ghost howling at the edges of this discourse. The haunting sound of bombs from the bloodiest century in human history sounds loudly at the borders of this new war. Our own bombs obliterating the other's body, destruction called democracy, death called freedom. On another morning, coffee in hand, I heard a man, interviewed on Paper Tiger TV, say, "If this [the WTC attack] is worse than Pearl Harbor then is what we are going to do worse than Hiroshima?" This is the sound of our own haunting history. Unfortunately, it will probably be a long time before the death count in Afghanistan reaches CNN. Yet the bombs dropped in our name, seen through low-tech monochrome less sophisticated than current video games, and the detention of Middle Eastern bodies are both spurred on by the discourse of Anthrax and the fear created over an infected body America.

### NOTES

1. This essay is about the emergence of the discourse. As such, it is bound to a particular moment in time—namely, the period between the beginning of October 2001 and the middle of November 2001. Therefore, it is quite possible that the discourse of Anthrax could shift and change in the next several months and years.

2. George Lakoff, "Metaphor and War: The Metaphor System Used to Justify War in the Gulf," *Vietnam Generation Journal and Newsletter,* vol. 3, no. 3 (1991).

3. By synecdochic doubling I mean that the one person comes to represent the entirety of a group and the entirety of a group is represented in the one person. In so doing, I am using a literary term in a social manner. As in poetry or other literary forms wherein a part comes to represent the whole and vice versa, discrimination, I argue, functions in a similar manner.

4. My discussion of the discourses of HIV and its association with the gay male body addresses the earliest discourse surrounding HIV/AIDS. This discourse shifted with the large social and political work of groups such as ACT-UP and Queer Nation. Moreover, as more straight bodies (specifically hemophiliacs) became HIV seropositive, the discourse surrounding HIV began to change.

5. A cultural panic is a type of anxiety attack that functions on a social level wherein the population is stirred into a frenzy over something that could potentially happen to the American people. Since 9/11 the cultural panic over Anthrax has been perpetuated by discourses of the media and the U.S. government.

6. *Watertown Daily Times,* October 26, 2001: 1.

### SUGGESTIONS FOR FURTHER READING

Douglas, Mary. *Purity and Danger: An Analysis of Concepts of Pollution and Taboo.* Harmondsworth: Penguin, 1970.

Foucault, Michel. *Discipline and Punish: The Birth of the Prison.* New York: Vintage Books, 1995.

Gooding-Williams, Robert, ed. *Reading Rodney King/Reading Urban Uprising.* New York: Routledge, 1993.

# 2. Blowback

PATRICIA M. THORNTON AND
THOMAS F. THORNTON

In the rush to make sense of the September 11 attacks and to understand their significance in national history, two major competing perspectives emerged in the American media. The first, put forth explicitly by the Bush Administration, emphasized that America was an innocent victim of historically unprecedented terrorist attacks by "evil" forces. The second, championed chiefly by critics of American foreign policy, viewed the fatal hijackings as "blowback," or unexpected, negative consequences on our country resulting from American imperialism and adventurism abroad. Significantly, these two perspectives contain radically opposing concepts of history and destiny, political responsibility, and moral obligation.

Early statements from the Bush White House were notable in their cautious restraint in terms of assigning culpability for the attacks, and focused on the uniqueness of the event in American history. Instead, the administration chose to frame the tragedy in terms of a moral conflict that cast the United States as a hapless victim of historical events that were not of its own making, but to which it must nonetheless respond. Standing in the National Cathedral at a service to commemorate the victims of the September 11 attacks, President Bush solemnly observed:

Just three days removed from these events, Americans do not yet have the distance of history. But our responsibility to history is already clear: to answer these attacks and rid the world of evil. . . . This conflict was begun on the timing and terms of others. It will end in a way, and at an hour, of our choosing.[1]

According to the Bush Administration, the "evil doers" responsible for the recent wave of attacks managed to hijack not only American airplanes, but also the nation's capacity to define itself as an agent of history. Cast as the hapless victim of an unprovoked attack, Bush and his supporters sought to chart a course for a future action that would restore the nation's rightful place in the world and ensure its destiny. Following this interpretation of events, the CNN headlines, which so neatly encapsulate the media metanarrative of events, soon switched from "America under Attack" to "America's New War."

Whereas the Bush White House seemed to frame the issue in moral terms and place it outside history, other observers saw the United States not as a blameless victim or a crusader of "good" against "evil," but rather as a victim of its own misguided foreign policy. In the immediate aftermath of September 11, a small group of American media pundits with a uniquely historical perspective pronounced the wave of terrorist assaults a prime example of the phenomenon of "blowback," a putative CIA term describing the unintended consequences of policy strategies that rebound on their makers. On September 12, the host of Chicago's public radio station WBEZ-FM interviewed Chalmers Johnson, founder of the Japan Policy Research Institute and author of *Blowback: The Costs and Consequences of American Empire.* Johnson referred to the events of the previous day as a "catastrophic failure" of U.S. intelligence and analysis that took Americans by surprise, as Pearl Harbor had decades earlier, in large part because they took so little interest in the history leading up to the event.[2] In an interview the following day, Johnson announced that he had not only seen the September 11 catastrophe coming, but that his book had in fact been "a warning to my fellow Americans, a year ago, that our foreign policy was going to produce something like this. It's important to stress, contrary to what people in Washington and the media are saying, that this was not an attack on the United States: this was an attack on American foreign policy."[3]

In the weeks that followed, discussions of Islamic "blowback" had become so prevalent in the press that by early October the *Guardian* listed "blowback" as a word "that should be banned." The London-based newspaper argued that, like "any new words made up by military men," "blowback" has "an extremely sinister intent":

> If you start using established words and phrases, you are laying yourself open to judgement by established codes of ethics, logics and good sense. But if you make up a new word, you don't just avoid setting off the triggers of censure, you also fashion yourself a jargon and thereby an air of expertise that makes people more circumspect about criticising you.

Furthermore, the *Guardian* pointed out, while the term "blowback" describes "the adverse consequences of a wartime decision that only came to light some time after that decision had been made . . . we already have heaps of ways in which to say 'that turned out to be completely the wrong thing to do.'" The one usage of the term "blowback" that the *Guardian* did not, however, object to was its "use by dopeheads, to describe the activity of putting a joint backwards into their mouths, affixing that mouth to someone else's, then cupping both hands around the mouth and blowing," observing wryly, "that really is a concept that needs its own word."[4]

Sinister and contraband connotations aside, prior to its deployment by military intelligence, the term "blowback" originally referred to either back pressure in an internal combustion or boiler, or the residue of gunpowder released upon the automatic ejection of a spent cartridge from a firearm. In scholarly discussions of strategic culture, "blowback" or "echo" refers to the process by which political and military decision makers initially invoke particular images or strategic symbols in order to win support for a particular course of action, but ultimately internalize their own instrumental rhetoric in a manner that constrains future decision making.[5] Similarly, Christopher Simpson, who in 1988 also published a book entitled *Blowback*, argued that in the wake of World War II the CIA, the U.S. State Department, and Army intelligence knowingly hired literally thousands of Nazi war criminals and their collaborators who were experts in propaganda, psychological warfare, and advanced weapons development. American officials had hoped that the former Nazis would give them a much-needed edge in their struggle to contain the Soviet Union in the postwar era. However, the operatives carried with them the dangerous baggage of Nazi "liberationism" to the American intelligence community. Ultimately, Simpson argued, the deployment of these Nazis as American operatives served to both deepen and intensify the Cold War by infecting the postwar intelligence community in the United States with "an implacable paranoia toward the USSR that would permit no arms control treaties, no trade and indeed no East-West cooperation of any type, only relentless preparation for war."[6]

Blowback's formal adoption into the vocabulary of "spook-speak," according to Johnson, dates to a recently declassified March 1954 CIA report on the operation to overthrow the rule of Mohammed Mossadegh in Iran that took place the previous year. Expressing concern that their intensive undercover meddling in

Iranian affairs might provoke some sort of retaliatory action against the United States in the future, the CIA appears to have predicted the chain of events that followed. The anticipated "blowback" came in 1979, when, after twenty-five years of repression at the hands of the U.S.–backed Shah, the Iranian Revolution replaced him with the Ayatollah Khomeini, inaugurating a new, virulently anti-American regime in Iran.[7] Other examples of "blowback" cited by Johnson include the 1988 bombing of Pan Am 103 over Lockerbie, Scotland, in apparent retaliation for an aerial assault on Libya two years before that took the life of Muammar Khadafi's stepdaughter; the explosion of cocaine and heroin addiction in American inner cities over the past two decades, partially the result of military officials and corrupt politicians, originally trained and cultivated by the CIA and then installed in power in various Central and South American regimes; and the August 1998 bombings of American embassy buildings in Nairobi and Dar es Salaam in apparent retribution for the stationing of American troops in Saudi Arabia during and after the Persian Gulf War.[8]

Johnson concluded his study with an assertion that now appears, in the wake of September 11, almost eerie in its prescience:

> "Blowback" is shorthand for saying that a nation reaps what it sows, even if it does not fully know or understand what it has sown. Given its wealth and power, the United States will be a prime recipient in the foreseeable future of all of the more expectable forms of blowback, particularly terrorist attacks against Americans in and out of the armed forces anywhere on earth, including within the United States.[9]

In interviews since September 11, Johnson has identified the emergence of the Taliban in Afghanistan and its support of terrorist cells as "blowback" for American patronage of the Afghan rebellion that expelled the Soviet troops in 1989. During the decade of Soviet occupation, over a million Afghans lost their lives in the bloody struggle, which was actively encouraged by the CIA and abetted by Pakistan's Inter-Services Intelligence (ISI) agency, which sought to turn the Afghan struggle into a global *jihad* enlisting all Muslim states against the Soviets. Bin Laden, a wealthy Saudi cum Muslim ascetic, emerged as a key recruiter in this effort during the war. By 1984, bin Laden had control over a front organization known as the Maktab al-Khidamat (MAK), the primary function of which was to funnel money, arms, and fighters from the larger Muslim world into the Afghan war. Many of these Muslim volunteers, known collectively as the *mujahideen*, were trained and armed by CIA operatives, sometimes working in concert with the Pakistani ISI. The goal of these covert operations was not merely to defeat and expel the invading Soviet forces, but to do so in a way that drew the conflict out over a long period of time and frittered away Soviet resources to the greatest extent possible (saddling them with "their own Vietnam," as it were). To that end, covert American support of a fratricidal alliance of seven Afghan resistance groups ultimately totaled more than three billion dollars.[10]

Following the expulsion of Soviet troops, bin Laden left Afghanistan and returned to his family business, but not before breaking with the MAK and forming a new group named al-Qaeda from the more extreme elements associated with the MAK. Yet less than three years after the Soviet withdrawal, the government in Kabul finally fell to the *mujahideen* who had driven out the Russians. A bloody civil war erupted, partially fueled by neighboring countries seeking to carve out areas of influence within the war-torn nation. The subsequent conflict pit the majority Pashtun peoples of the south and east against those based in the north, including the Tajik, Uzbek, Hazara, and Turkmen ethnic minorities. Precisely at this key juncture, previously generous U.S. assistance to the Afghan groups slowed to a trickle, and by 1994 all but ceased.[11]

Into this vacuum came the Pashtun-backed Taliban, espousing a program of reform and heavily supported by Pakistan's ISI during the rule of Prime Minister Benazir Bhutto. With extremist religious commitments that might not have otherwise attracted much support in conservative but traditionally tolerant Afghanistan, the Taliban promised peace to the war-torn populace. Yet the end of civil strife came with a high price for both those inside and outside Afghanistan. The *mujahideen* turned their wrath against not only many of the residents of the nation they had originally enlisted to defend, but also against their U.S. and Pakistani backers. Al-Qaeda operatives have since been linked to not only the September 11 attacks but also to the bombing of the USS Cole and of two American embassies in Kenya and Tanzania. In Pakistan, they are suspected of having plotted assassination attempts against General Musharraf.

For critics of American foreign policy, "blowback" is a manifestation of the still largely unacknowledged empire-building process that America undertook during the Cold War era; the CIA's abandonment of their protégés among the *mujahideen* once they lost their value as pawns in the Cold War is part of a long-established pattern in the history of American foreign policy. Similar scenarios, argue Johnson and others, have played out on numerous stages, like those in Liberia, Somalia, and Congo. In each of the foregoing cases, seemingly bottomless wells of covert aid suddenly dried up as these remote locales ceased to entertain battles of interest to Cold Warriors, and in each case the subsequent descent into anarchy inaugurated new spasms of genocidal politics: the reign of Charles Taylor in Liberia, Mohamed Farah Aideed in Somalia, and the Hutu refugee camps of the Congo.[12]

Johnson stresses that the roots of American "imperial overstretch" lie in its contest with the Soviet Union in the aftermath of World War II. In his analysis, the panoply of problems faced by U.S. policy makers today would simply not exist had it not been for the imperial commitments and operations that gave shape to the Cold War. A self-described former "spear-carrier for empire," Johnson readily admits that his own careers, both military and then academic, were largely funded and fueled by the dynamics of Soviet containment in East Asia. At the same time, he warns against the usual logics deployed by U.S. decision makers in the crafting of American foreign policy:

> The most common government argument for such continued imperialist activism in the wake of that half-century-long superpower confrontation is still a version of the old "domino theory," discredited during the Vietnam War: America's armed forces and covert warriors—for the sake of the world's good—have no choice but to hold off "instability" wherever it may threaten. . . . But instability, a nebulous concept at best, is the normal state of affairs in an international system of sovereign states. Instability as such does not threaten the security of the United States, particularly when there is no superpower rival eager to exploit it.[13]

But why is the United States feeling "blowback" so strongly now? One reason is that the United States has emerged as the only superpower and thus has become the focal point of resistance for those opposed to its influence and meddling. A second reason is the process of globalization itself. Globalization has vastly increased the interconnectedness and interdependence of states through the increased volume and speed of human, capital, communication, and transportation flows. Indeed, the nation-state has become much less of a "container" with firm borders than a nexus of flows with permeable boundaries. Within this new world system, blowback can be characterized as a kind of negative feedback. In this sense the term also has an ecological connotation beyond the mechanics of internal combustion. We can expect negative feedback in the form of blowback and other resistance as long as the United States attempts to unilaterally control, dominate, or "stabilize" the world political system for its own short-term interests. As many analysts predict, Americans—both those enlisted in the military as well as average civilians going about their normal daily business—are likely to continue to serve as the targets of "blowback" in the future, the victims of retaliatory strikes for covert operations of which they have little or no knowledge. Whereas the American press and official rhetoric prefer to frame such attacks as isolated incidents, the unjust attacks of "rogue nations," it is also possible, by carefully sifting through the evidence of history, that such victims were made by the covert actions of American military operatives. The shock and suddenness of such attacks tend to obscure the fact that horrific acts of terror may be linked to systemic failures in American foreign policy.

"Blowback" itself is an obscuring, impersonal piece of language. Thus, like nuclear "fallout" and "collateral damage," the ostensible purpose underlying the term is to conceal the brutal realities of war from the curious gaze of uninitiated civilians back home who must nonetheless be counted on to support military efforts—both overt and covert—abroad. Taxpayers who fund the development of weapons of mass destruction might prefer to contemplate only indirectly—if at all—the fact that nuclear explosions rain down a fine silt of carcinogens on the citizens of other countries for weeks following a nuclear explosion. Innocent civilians who happen into the paths of bombs intended for military targets represent an unintended cost of war that homeland populations are encouraged not to calculate as they move about the business of their daily lives.

"Blowback" also represents an uncomfortable category of military realities with which the majority of U.S. citizens remain for the most part unaware. The covert pursuit of American interests abroad has often led to the cementing of distinctly unpalatable alliances with individuals and groups whose behavior and goals would surely win few, if any, supporters among the domestic population. These deals with the devil are nonetheless, we are collectively assured, necessary to safeguard our long-term interests abroad. Thus, "blowback" becomes part of the dehumanized cant of America's imperial wars, suggestive more of accident and happenstance than the exaction of some alien notion of justice by brutally calculated design.

This reading of recent events is indeed a bitter pill for most Americans to swallow. Perhaps popular ignorance and widespread naiveté regarding the brutal facts of war are a necessary screen for most Americans. The Bush Administration's projection of the events of September 11 into a realm where history is forgotten in the ready embrace of abstract moral imperatives—responsibility, duty, and justice—may well prove the more comforting national fiction. As Nietzsche reflected upon the German historical imagination a century ago,

> Cheerfulness, the good conscience, the joyful deed, confidence in the future—all of them depend, in the case of the individual as of a nation, on the existence of a line dividing the bright and discernible from the unilluminable and dark; on one's being just as able to forget at the right time as to remember at the right time; on the possession of a powerful instinct for sensing when it is necessary to feel historically and when unhistorically. This, precisely, is the proposition the reader is invited to meditate upon: the unhistorical and the historical are necessary in equal measure for the health of an individual, of a people, and of a culture.[14]

While it is understandable that the U.S. government should respond to the carnage of September 11 by positing a clear "dividing line" between the "bright" forces of civilization and the "dark" forces of terrorism, we would argue, with Nietzsche, that a historical perspective is necessary in equal measure for the future health of the United States within the community of nations. To this end, it is important to critically interrogate the phenomenon of blowback. For even though the disastrous consequences of blowback are by definition unintended, within a historical and political-ecological context they are more explicable and predictable than the hapless victim perspective suggests. More importantly, by understanding the root causes of past and present blowback, including U.S. hegemony, unilateralism, and "imperial overstretch," it may be possible to avoid instances of this phenomenon in the future.

**NOTES**

1. Office of the Press Secretary, "President's Remarks at National Day of Prayer and Remembrance," September 14, 2001.

2. Video Monitoring Services of America, "Worldview" (September 12, 2001), WBEZ-FM interview with Chalmers Johnson.

3. Jeff Shaw, "What Goes Around Comes Around: An Interview with Chalmers Johnson," *In These Times*, October 29, 2001: 18.

4. Zoe Williams, "Words That Should Be Banned (25): Blowback," *The Guardian* (London), October 6, 2001: 7.

5. Alastair Iain Johnston, "Thinking about Strategic Culture," *International Security* 19:4 (Spring 1995): 58, n. 55; Jack Snyder, *Myths of Empire: Domestic Politics and International Ambition* (Ithaca: Cornell University Press, 1991), 42; Richard Rosencrance, "The Vulnerability of Empire," *International Security* 19:4 (Spring 1995): 143.

6. Christopher Simpson, *Blowback: America's Recruitment of Nazis and Its Effects on the Cold War* (New York: Weidenfeld and Nicholson, 1988), 277.

7. "Blowback: U.S. Actions Abroad Have Repeatedly Led to Unintended, Indefensible Consequences," *Nation*, October 15, 2001: 13.

8. Chalmers Johnson, *Blowback: The Costs and Consequences of American Empire* (New York: Henry Holt and Company, 2000), 8–10.

9. Johnson, *Blowback*, 223.

10. Mary Ann Weaver, "Blowback," *Atlantic Monthly* 277:5 (May 1996): 24–36.

11. Peter Beinhart, "Back to Front," *New Republic* (October 8, 2001).

12. Beinhart, "Back to Front."

13. Johnson, *Blowback*, 29.

14. Friedrich Nietzsche, "On the Uses and Disadvantages of History for Life," *Untimely Meditations*, translated by R. J. Hollingdale (Cambridge: Cambridge University Press, 1983), 63.

## SUGGESTIONS FOR FURTHER READING

Barber, Benjamin, and Andrea Schulz, eds. *Jihad vs. McWorld: How Globalism and Tribalism Are Reshaping the World.* New York: Ballantine, 1996.

Borovik, Artem. *The Hidden War: A Russian Journalist's Account of the Soviet War in Afghanistan.* New York: Grove Press, 2001.

Gowan, Peter. *The Global Gamble: Washington's Faustian Bid for World Dominance.* London: Verso, 1999.

Johnson, Chalmers. *Blowback: The Costs and Consequences of American Empire.* New York: Henry Holt and Company, 2000.

Simpson, Christopher. *Blowback: America's Recruitment of Nazis and Its Effects on the Cold War.* New York: Weidenfeld and Nicholson, 1988.

# 3. Civilization versus Barbarism

Marina A. Llorente

"Civilization under attack" has been one of the headlines used by the news media to describe the events of September 11, 2001. During the initial days when the perpetrators were not officially known, the missing subject of the headline ("under attack" by whom?) was often filled in, for consumers of the media, by the word "barbarism." Several questions arise from this mechanical assumption. How does the concept of "civilization" bring to mind the concept of "barbarism"? What is meant by "civilization" and "barbarism" in this context? How does the opposition between "civilization" and "barbarism" work so effectively? Finally, for what ends and by whom has the dichotomy been employed after September 11?

In order to answer these questions, one has to look first at the binary structure of language. Almost every noun, adjective, adverb, and verb has its opposite; usually this opposition implies a devaluation of one term and a favoring of the other. The assumption of inequality between the two terms goes without question; one is lacking something that the opposite embodies. Man/Woman, Good/Evil, Urban/Rural, Primitive/Modern, and West/East are well-known examples of the way this binary system works. In the case of (Western) Civilization/(Eastern) Barbarism, the last term is the devalued one. The story of how

"barbarism" became the devalued term in relation to "civilization" is, in fact, the story of how the powerful nations of "the
West" came to exert their cultural, political, economic, and military domination over the rest of the world.

Language, in other words, is closely related to history and politics. It is a long story as ancient as the binary structure of language itself, but it is also a story of social constructions, a story of
powers that need to be deconstructed and dismantled. As a
philologist myself, I know very well about the impossibility of getting rid of the binary system. The system, after all, determines the
way a word is understood in relation to other words; it is a system
of oppositions. What this system does not do is to devalue one
term in relation to the opposite one; that is the work of the dominant ideology in a specific moment in a specific place. What we
need to do, then, is to trace language backward and be aware of
where, how, and by whom abstract nouns such as "West" and
"East," "civilization" and "barbarism" have been created, and how
they have been used in the days following September 11.

Before the story of these opposed social constructs is laid out,
it is useful to start by analyzing the recent statements of politicians who rely on the "civilization/barbarism" dichotomy. U.S.
Secretary of State Colin Powell was one of the first officials to invoke the idea that "civilization" was being confronted; in his own
words, terrorists were "attacking civilization." President Bush also
referred to the terrorists as "those barbaric people who attacked
our country." In another statement from Camp David, Bush said
"a group of barbarians has declared war," and declared that the
United States would therefore wage "a new kind of war, a struggle against barbarians." He ended by stating that the country
"needs to win a war against barbaric behavior."

The discourse of both Powell and Bush demonstrates a clear,
binary opposition between one part of the world, the "civilized"
United States and Europe, against the other part, the irrational

people from "barbaric" and undeveloped eastern countries with "uncivilized" traditions, costumes, and cultural practices. Through the use of this dichotomy, we are asked to believe that the behavior of these new "barbarians" is uncontrollably guided by the same cruel instincts that motivated some of the most infamous "barbarians" of past centuries, including Attila the Hun and the Mongol leader Genghis Khan. From the moment that Powell and Bush categorized the perpetrators of the attack as "barbarians," the enemies of "America's new war" were directly linked with the legends of other enemies whose existence predates the United States itself, and with the image of menacing nomadic armies coming on horseback to conquer fifth or fourteenth century Europe. Within this discourse, the men who attacked the World Trade Center towers and the Pentagon are the postmodern Attila or Genghis Khan, using their flying horses to devastate the two symbols—one economic, the other military—that are the basis of the current civilized world. In their early statements, the president and his secretary of state were preparing their audiences for the war they were going to declare.

Later on, as the events unfolded and the war was already in progress, the president again echoed Powell, using the concept of "civilization" in a speech given at the Asia-Pacific Economic Cooperation on October 20 in Shanghai, China. It is worth mentioning that during the fifth century, China, in an effort to stop the conquest of its territory by barbarians, built the Great Wall, the longest wall on earth. The Chinese historically were one of the civilizations that battled successfully against the barbaric Mongolian hordes that wanted to conquer and seize the economic power of the Chinese empire. What the president did in his speech in Shanghai, then, was to address the "civilized" Asiatic countries as allies against the "barbaric" terrorists, making an implicit reference to the history of China itself. In fact, the message of the president can be read as follows: The United States and its allies in the project of economic globalization, among them China, are fighting the barbarians/terrorists in the same way that China did in the fifth century. The place once occupied by the Chinese empire has been taken by the American empire.

Obviously there are several layers in this message. First is the implied notion of China joining the United States in fighting back the barbarian hordes. In regard to this point, President Bush said, "We are deeply grateful to countries—including all the APEC [Asia-Pacific Economic Cooperation] countries—that have now joined in a great coalition against terror." The same APEC countries, it should be noted, have successfully joined the U.S.–led coalition of the process of globalization as well. Second, but intimately related to the first, is the powerful economic discourse of globalization taking over all these Asian countries, a discourse that the president was explicitly deploying throughout the speech. Unity in the war against terror was explicitly linked with unity in sharing the discourse of free trade and growth. As Bush put it, "We share more than a common enemy, we share a common goal: to expand our ties of trade and trust." In fact, as this essay was being written, China became a member of the World Trade Organization (WTO) over the objections of activists who decried China's record on human rights.

Before stating his economic message, President Bush started by offering a harangue in favor of unity against the terrorists: "The attacks of September 11th were really an attack on all civilized countries," he insisted, adding that "those who hate civilization and culture and progress cannot be appeased." By using a clear reference to the "appeasement" of Germany before the onset of World War II, Bush carefully linked the "barbaric" bin Laden with Hitler, with both men occupying the same uncivilized space of dishonest murderers. Following this line of thought, Bush immediately stated, "This conflict is a fight to save the civilized world, and nowhere do civilized people rejoice in the murder of children or the creation of orphans." Moreover, according to the president, the terrorists "have divorced themselves from the values that define civilization: openness, trade, and tolerance that produce prosperity, liberty and knowledge" as opposed to choosing "isolation, envy and resentment that produce poverty, stagnation and ignorance." In other words, if all the APEC countries choose more trade and not less openness, they will have prosperous economies, strong democracies, and wise citizens. Finally, the president made his economic discourse even more explicit: "The base of the prosperity is the economic progress that begins with freer trade that brings economic advancement and generates opportunity enhancing entrepreneur growth," and "the habits of economic freedom will create expectations of greater democracy." On the one hand, then, we have economic growth, and on the other the union against terrorism and the possibility of the development of democratic systems in the whole area.

The artificial dichotomy between "(Western) democratic civilization" and "(Eastern) totalitarian civilization" is clearly present in this speech. The first of these concepts, in Bush's view, embodies freedom, democracy, good, and wealth, while the second is characterized by the lack of freedom, totalitarian governments, evil, and poverty. This political rhetoric has been used, by the president and others, without being subject to serious questioning. Let's begin to deconstruct it. A good place to start is with the work of Edward Said, one of the most important intellectuals of our time. Said has explored how Western notions about culture articulated in literary texts, political discourse, and the media have served to perpetuate Western imperialism in general and, more recently, the imperial power of the United States. In his well-known book *Orientalism*, Said argues that the Western person is what he or she is only as long as there is an Eastern or "Oriental" one to compare or contrast with. The West exists, in other words, because the East does; one cannot exist without the other, because the defining characteristic of each is that it is not the other. On one side of the dichotomy is "the West," the "civilized world," the one that has the economic power, and on the other side is the powerless, "uncivilized world."

There are at least two problems with this notion. First, not everyone who lives in "the West" actually has the stereotypical lifestyle associated with that of "civilization." Instead, there are elites in every single country in the world, including the relatively poor countries of "the East," who have this kind of lifestyle. The fact that the general standard of living is higher in the United States than elsewhere does not take away from the fact that there exists a global economic elite. Second, the very idea of "the West" is a social construct. What do we mean when we speak of "the West"? What is the origin of the term? The term has existed for as long as "the East" has existed; the two give their respective meanings to each other, because they constitute a binary construction. "West" is everything that "East" is not, and vice versa. As noted above, however, "East" is clearly the devalued term in this pair.

A long series of historians have perpetuated ideas about the barbaric life, creating an entire culture's imagination of the barbarians. According to this history, as well as medieval folklore and tradition, Attila the Hun and Genghis Khan are the representatives of the barbarians who revolted against the empires of their respective eras. The barbarians were nomads and mounted warriors who did not play by the rules, in a military sense. Attila (406–453 A.D.) was a king and a general of the Huns, while Genghis Khan (1167–1227 A.D.) was the "Universal Ruler" who vigorously organized the Mongols into a formidable military force through conscription and the taking of tribute. Both men were great military innovators and did have armies that consisted of perhaps the best trained horsemen in human history. With these ferocious armies they conquered and terrorized significant portions of their respective worlds. Legends say that the Huns were known as the "Scourge of God" and that Attila dabbled in cannibalistic practices. Genghis Khan was no less threatening; he could move troops around in the heat of battle as easily as he would move chess pieces. Both of them were ruthless toward people who resisted the advances of their armies. If a town or city fought back, they would lay siege to it and, at the conclusion, exterminate its inhabitants. When news of these tactics spread, their armies successfully took over towns that would surrender at the first sight of the "barbarian" army. Thus the Huns and Mongols spread their terror across Asia and Europe. This is the history President Bush and other politicians and commentators invoke with words such as "barbaric behavior" or "uncivilized attack" (is there such a thing as a "civilized attack"?). These postmodern barbarians are attacking the global empire that is centered in the United States. Bin Laden, following in the footsteps of guerrilla armies past, does not follow the dominant rules of war set by the global empire that is centered in the United States; instead, he has chosen to use different tactics that may, in fact, constitute a totally new concept of war.

To study the barbaric nowadays is to enter an exotic world which is also a familiar world. In Freudian terms, "barbarians" are our id force, libidinous, irrational, violent, dangerous. Nevertheless, these characteristics are not seen as the norm in the Western person but only in the unknown Eastern person. Even the most violent acts of Westerners tend not to be labeled "barbaric." A good example is the case of Oklahoma City bomber Timothy McVeigh, whose action was not categorized in terms of "barbarism," presumably because he belonged to the "civilized" part of the world. In summary, the rational population in the West, with its instincts well-controlled, is the norm and is empowered, whereas the violent East is not. Hence the West is necessary to expose a shared illusion, namely, the supposed existence of a representative barbaric East as opposed to a monolithic, unified, powerful West. Nevertheless, the West is an abstraction because there is not a real entity (such as a nation-state) where the power of the West actually resides. Instead, there is a web of governments, transnational corporations, and financial institutions who decide the economic future of our world, and there is a policing, military, and imprisoning state that rules over us.

In this light, the concepts of freedom and democracy can be viewed as illusions as well. The current U.S. citizen is not a free person; he or she only believes he or she is a free human being in a supposedly democratic system. The term "civilized" and its opposite, "barbaric," have been employed by politicians to cover this reality—the lack of freedom and democracy and the existence of structured poverty, all over the world, including in the United States—while the real focus of power is on the development of "free trade" and the expansion of global capitalism. The term "civilized," in other words, is used to mobilize people in the projects of globalization, free trade, entrepreneurial growth—in short, the path of global economic progress that President Bush invoked in his speech in Shanghai.

Hidden within all this is a real struggle, not between "civilization" and "barbarism," but rather between powerful elites (including some members of the middle class, depending on the country) and the powerless people of the world, once again including those in the United States. As Orhan Pamuk stated in a November 15 article, and as critics of globalization have been arguing for years, "at no time in history has the gulf between rich and poor been so wide."[1] The fact that discussion of this issue has been displaced by a rhetoric of "civilization versus barbarism" can be traced to particular aspects of political discourse in the United States. Specifically, the narrative of "(Western) civilization" (powerful states) versus "(Eastern) barbarism" (powerless states) was redefined, ultimately in economic terms, during the last decade by Samuel P. Huntington, professor of International Politics at Harvard University. In his 1993 article "The Clash of Civilizations?"—later to become a well-known and much-quoted book—Huntington argues that at the end of the twentieth century and the beginning of the new millennium, "a civilization is the highest cultural grouping of people and the broadest level of cultural identity people have short of that which distinguishes humans from other species. It is defined both by common objective elements, such as language, history, religion, customs, institutions, and by the subjective self-identification of people."[2] Huntington distinguishes between eight civilizations in the current world: Western, Confucian, Japanese, Islamic, Hindu, Slavic-Orthodox, Latin American, and (in a seemingly racist move) "possibly" African. The people of different civilizations, he says, have different views on the relations between God and man, the individual and the group, the citizen and the state, parents and children, husband and wife, as well as differing views on the relative importance of rights and responsibilities, liberty and authority, equality and hierarchy.

The most interesting part of Huntington's argument, for the purpose of this essay, is that detailing the differences between "Western" and "Eastern" civilization: the first is Christian (Protestant or Catholic), has the common experiences of European history (feudalism, the Renaissance, the Reformation, the Enlightenment, the French Revolution, the Industrial Revolution), is economically better off than the "East," and may now look forward to increasing involvement in a common European economy and the consolidation of democratic political systems. The "East," by contrast, is Orthodox or Muslim, has historically belonged to the Ottoman or Tsarist empires, is only lightly touched by the shaping events in the rest of Europe, and, finally, seems much less likely to develop stable democratic political systems.

But what Huntington is missing here, as Edward Said has pointed out, is the crucial reliance of the Renaissance on "Eastern" culture and, more generally, the deep interdependence of supposedly separate "civilizations" throughout history. During the end of the Middle Ages, for example, a host of master narratives were translated in the Spanish court of Alfonso X, the Learned, by a well-prepared group of translators. The most important cultural texts written in Arabic, Greek, Latin, and Hebrew, among other languages, were translated into different Romance languages for the future Renaissance world, making it possible for European intellectuals to have access to the richness of the ancient world—and to claim all these texts as elements of an exclusively "Western" civilization. Thus the West owes its "civilized" culture, in part, to the East; the same could be said of Western technology, for without the knowledge contained in all those translations the West would never have accomplished all the progress that is now enjoyed by elites and middle classes in every part of the world.

More directly relevant to the events of September 11 and the subsequent U.S. "war on terrorism," Said has also persuasively argued that Huntington's article was intended to supply Americans with an original thesis about "a new phase" in world politics after the end of the Cold War. Huntington—whose earlier theories helped shape U.S. policy during the Cold War—does exactly this. His binary opposition is not the former one between "civilization" and "barbarism," since he argues that there is not one civilization, but rather several sharply differing civilizations. Instead, underlying his argument is the existence of another binary opposition: the West, constituted by the elites and middle classes who enjoy the benefits of capitalism and globalization, and the Rest of the world, constituted by those who generally resent the domination of the West. Huntington shrewdly admits that "the Rest" may have some legitimate grievances against "the West," including U.S. domination of the UN Security Council, the problematic policies of the IMF and World Bank, and the history of U.S. military intervention abroad. In the end, however, he still provides his readers with a new enemy: "several Islamic-Confucian states" whose "expansion" must be limited by the United States, in alliance with those "whose cultures are close to those of the West." In summary, for Huntington, the old binary is still in place but has been modified: on one side there is the United States (leader of the West), and on the other side is anyone who opposes U.S. hegemony.

Huntington's arguments have been permeating the narratives of international politics during the last decade, and we can see their imprint on President Bush's aforementioned speech in Shanghai. The president based the concept of "civilized world" (Western, Latin American, and Japanese civilizations plus China) on globalization, a world economic system, arguing that this is partly what was attacked by terrorists on September 11. To prove that it was an attack on all the "civilized" world, he listed the many different nationalities of those killed and missing in the attacks, then pointed out how after the attack, everyone in the "civilized" world came back to the steady work of building the market-based economic system that "has brought more prosperity more quickly to more people than at any time in human history because they have followed the rules of the modern world, the progress of trade and freedom." The old "(Western) civilization" has expanded economically to include a group of civilizations that share the same economic interest in free trade and entrepreneurial growth, creating a coalition of "civilized," powerful elites opposed to the "barbaric," powerless population of the world where terrorists of all classes and types have found their home.

The reality, however, is not all that simple. I agree with Orhan Pamuk that if powerless citizens of every single country in the world, including the United States, are questioning U.S. policy in light of the September 11 attacks, it is not because they are fundamentalists, or because of the trumpeted clash between "East" and "West," or even (or not only) because of their poverty. It is the feeling of impotence deriving from degradation, the failure to be understood, and the inability of such people to make their voices heard that leads them to ask the "why" question that has been so carefully avoided within the United States. This is the real challenge that the "civilized" world is confronting at this moment in time. It is not, as President Bush put it at the end of his speech in Shanghai, "the time to act boldly, to build and defend an age of liberty." Liberty, freedom, and progress for what and for whom? To act boldly, repeatedly bombing Afghanistan, and to continue building and defending the process of globalization that will make the rich, "civilized," "democratic" people richer?

The eternal binary is still in place. The old "West" has become nominally democratic and inclusive for economic reasons and the old "East" has become undemocratic and exclusive for economic reasons as well, and both halves of the binary have been globalized. All of us, citizens of the so-called "civilized" world, must confront our uncomfortable reality after September 11. Is it not paradoxical to select defending freedom and democracy when the members of the Senate and the Congress have renounced, for an undefined period of time, their right to act as a check on the power of the executive, the military, and the CIA? We have been without democracy for a while. We have not had real freedom either, but now we know. September 11 has put the plain truth in front of us on the screen in our living rooms, because when the two towers fell down, so too did the illusion of the democracy. This is our "civilized" call. Let's begin recovering our democratic voice in the Senate and the Congress and let's hear the "barbaric" voices of the damned starting, finally, a dialogue where the powerful civilized citizens of the elites from the whole world will be the silent interlocutors and the powerless civilized citizens of every country in the world, including the United States, will express themselves freely and largely.

## NOTES

1. Orhan Pamuk, "The Anger of the Damned," translated by Mary Isin, *New York Review of Books,* November 15, 2001.

2. Samuel P. Huntington, "The Clash of Civilizations?" *Foreign Affairs,* Summer 1993.

## SUGGESTIONS FOR FURTHER READING

Bury, John B. *The Invasion of Europe by the Barbarians.* New York: W. W. Norton, 2000.

Coetzee, J. M. *Waiting for the Barbarians.* New York: Penguin Books, 1999.

Culler, Jonathan. *On Deconstruction: Theory and Criticism after Structuralism.* Ithaca: Cornell University Press, 1982.

Derrida, Jacques. *Writing and Difference.* Translated by Allan Bass. Chicago: University of Chicago Press, 1978.

Said, Edward W. *Culture and Imperialism.* New York: Vintage Books, 1994.

———. *Orientalism.* New York: Pantheon, 1978.

Ross Glover, *Steroids for Dummies. Reprinted with the permission of Ross Glover.*

# 4. Cowardice

R. DANIELLE EGAN

On the night of September 11, as images of planes crashing into buildings replayed endlessly, images imprinted on the American memory forever, the term "coward" entered into the public discourse as a way to help people make sense of how nineteen men could hijack three planes and take the lives of so many in New York, Washington, D.C., and Pennsylvania. Stunned by such an atrocity, one that seemed like the things of which nightmares are made, governmental and media discourses promoted the notion of cowardice to fill the void which, for many, was beyond words. To reclaim our position of strength, George W. Bush threw down the gauntlet in his speech on 9/11 when he said, "Make no mistake, the United States will hunt down and punish those responsible for these cowardly acts. The resolve of our great nation is being tested. But make no mistake: we will show the world that we can pass the test. God bless."

However, is cowardice the right term? Is suicide bombing cowardly or is it something else? What options are immediately excluded by invoking such a term? I am not arguing that the acts of 9/11 were in any way justified; however, I do want to argue that by invoking the term coward, a clearly emasculating term, the U.S. government made bombing Afghanistan inevitable and other forms of resolution unthinkable.

Using cowardice as a metaphor for the attacks of 9/11 constructs a gendered discourse that foregrounds masculinity as a way to help understand 9/11 and as a justification for the bombing in Afghanistan. In this discourse, a coward is less than a man, one who does things underhandedly and either refuses to fight or plays dirty when he engages in a fight. The coward is not man enough to say it to your face and instead chooses to say it behind your back. In essence the coward is the antithesis of the dominant ideology of masculinity in a patriarchal culture. Adjectives such as strong, rational, aggressive, and brave describe masculinity, while femininity is viewed as weak, irrational, passive, and cowardly. The coward does not fit into the above descriptions of masculinity and can be associated with the sissy, the pussy, the pansy, and other derogatory terms which associate men with the feminine as opposed to the masculine. To be called a coward is to have one's masculinity questioned. The discourses used by the U.S. government and the media create a binary wherein on the one side you have the coward and on the other you have the hero who must do something to teach the coward a lesson. When George W. Bush uses the phrase "cowardly acts of the terrorists," he is basically asking the coward to fight like a man. In so doing, the opponent who is deemed a coward is supposed to do one of two things—come and fight or run away.

The discourse of the coward erases complexity, flattening both parties into binaries of man and not-man (thus feminine). Moreover, it functions to background the clearly inhumane actions of our "heroic-manly" attacks in Afghanistan in our attempt to make our freedom endure. All actions of the hero become necessary and valiant efforts to defend the victim—the United States. This is not to say that there should have been no response to the attacks, but it does mean that a complex ethical response is automatically foreclosed (see "Justice" in this volume). Although extradition was discussed, it was couched as a demand:

"Give up bin Laden or else." The ultimatum would make the Taliban lose face, a form of emasculation that is often invoked in fights between men. The World Court, which has handled cases involving some of the most heinous human rights abusers, such as the Serbian war criminals from the Bosnian war, was beyond real consideration. The discourse of the coward also makes it impossible for us not to fight back with military force lest we become the cowards. The bombs had to be dropped. The coward would pay.

The discourse of the coward, far from only defining the men who actually hijacked the planes on 9/11, is extended to the Taliban, Osama bin Laden, and anyone else who is against us, thereby justifying our attacks. On October 9, 2001 the *Globe*[1] printed a story stating, "in a chilling affirmation that the cowardly attack on the United States was an act of pure evil this amazing photo of the blasted World Trade Center towers captures the hideous face of the devil himself." In addition, the *Globe* article claims, "some eyewitnesses even say the eerie image bears a resemblance to terrorist mastermind and prime suspect Osama Bin Laden." This story makes those involved not only cowards but evil as well, a historically feminine trait. One need look no farther than biblical references to Eve and her tasting of the forbidden fruit to recognize the historical connections of femininity to evil. By linking the cowardly bin Laden with evil, a violent response is justified, not unlike the way judges in seventeenth-century America justified burning women at the stake, although these women at least received a hearing.

The discourse of the coward promotes our hero sweeping in to quell cowardly acts, wherever they might crop up. In so doing, this discourse also tries to stifle dissent. Who, after all, would want to criticize a hero? This is evidenced in the termination of Bill Maher's contract. The host of the ABC television talk show, *Politically Incorrect*, had the audacity to say, "We have been the cowards, lobbing cruise missiles from 2,000 miles away. That's cowardly. Staying in the airplane when it hits the building—say what you want about it, it's not cowardly." Maher, who is far from a radical leftist—he has espoused controversial opinions on prostitution and feminism and on the legalization of drugs, to the chagrin of liberals and conservatives alike—was immediately sanctioned for his speech (a freedom, one would suppose, we are trying to protect) and made to apologize. However, to question the hero and, more importantly, to problematize the discourse of the coward, was too damaging and the network is currently looking for a new host. This is further shown in the case of the man in West Virginia who was arrested for wearing a T-shirt that read "U.S. out of Afghanistan."

The mainstream media sources, through their virtual lack of serious attention to protests in the United States and among our allies, particularly after the initial bombing began, serve to make dissent invisible and to represent a strong America, a hero who is fully supported at home and among our allies. The mainstream media perpetuates the discourse of the coward. In so doing, it supports policies which make it necessary to show that the coward is deserving of punishment when images of the hero's onslaught of bombing and its aftermath are covered by CNN. When the President of CNN stated that his reporters must, in effect, support the hero by "balancing" pictures of death and destruction in Afghanistan with descriptions of the evils of the enemy, this recapitulates the discourse of the coward to make sure the American people do not waver in their support of both the hero and his methods.

The need to protect the image of the hero is so prominent in both governmental and media discourses that it should make us wonder whether there are cracks in our hero's armor and whether his support could wane at any moment. Make no mistake about it, this is about masculinity. In the same October 9,

2001 issue of the *Globe*, bin Laden's masculinity and character were questioned and his cowardice made public alongside that of Saddam Hussein and Moammar Gadhafi, two other cowards the United States has had to confront in the past. The article stated that these men hate their people and their religion. They are, at base, not real men, they are hypocritical cowards who should be put in their place (which I assume, given our past policies, is in the ground) by the real man—George W. Bush. *The Tonight Show* with Jay Leno also portrays bin Laden as stupid and goofy, with spoofs on the making of the videos released by bin Laden. In these spoofs bin Laden gives away his location and makes endless other mistakes, all showing that he is inept, dumb, and will in essence be defeated because he is no real hero, he is no real man.[2] The interesting thing about the discourse of the coward is that it constructs the fight as if it is between two men—Bush versus bin Laden—when in fact these are two individuals who will probably never meet. In wartime, states metaphorically come to be represented as a particular person so that the "battle" is seen as between two individuals and not two militaries.[3] The original cowards are dead, so they become bin Laden and the Taliban; however, bin Laden comes to represent all these parties so that all cowardice is embodied in him, as the entire U.S. military comes to be represented in the man who sent them there, George W. Bush. This is, of course, highly contrary to the reality of war, where both parties must use stand-in cowards and stand-in heroes to fight their fight. In many ways both Bush and bin Laden are protected while the stand-ins, at least the stand-in cowards, are the ones whose lives will be lost.

With the sheer size of our military and the technological advances of our weapons, the whole idea of a fair fight between a hero and a coward becomes not only suspect, but also highly problematic. How can the military of one of the wealthiest and most technologically armed countries in the world have a fair fight with one of the poorest? How does dropping so-called "daisy cutter" bombs, which instantaneously incinerate a one-square-mile area, on Afghanistan—the people of which, our government reiterates endlessly, are not the targets of our attack—become particularly heroic? Why wasn't our masculinity reinstated in the first days or weeks of bombing? Why are the bombings continuing with more zeal and more strength (starting with smart bombs, then cluster bombs, and now daisy cutters), if this is a fair fight? What becomes obvious in the bombing which is taking the lives of innocent civilians, aid workers, and hospital workers is not heroics, but another form of masculinity—the bully.

With the inequity between the two sides one has to wonder if this is a war or whether, in fact, it is a systematic form of destruction of an enemy who can hardly fight back. Is it war when one side has the tools to virtually annihilate an enemy who has no ability to do anywhere near the same? To use a sports metaphor, if this were a boxing match could the continual bombing be represented as something like Mike Tyson versus a hundred-pound high school student? Is this not bullyism? Is this not hypermasculinity? We see this dynamic when images on CNN show proud soldiers writing the names of firefighter and policemen heroes on phallus-shaped bombs used to "penetrate" and "take over" enemy territory. We need to show "our strength," after all, and what better way to do it than with stand-in heroes in planes dropping penises into the dark holes within which cowards hide? Our "resolution," "determination," and masculinity will prevail. We will beat them into submission. In recent history the United States and its allies have fought other wars and conflicts with enemies who were almost defenseless—Grenada in the 1980s and Iraq in the 1990s are two that come to mind. However, war itself is a masculine endeavor and the metaphors and discourses surrounding it evoke masculine terms to make sense of both the need to go to war and the need to finish the job once we get there.

On November 8, 2001, George W. Bush said, "Let's roll!" The phrase emerged from a passenger on the plane which went down in Pennsylvania, but it is also often used on film when the hero goes to fight the good fight. Ironically, our country had been rolling on Afghanistan for over a month, supporting the Northern Alliance leader, General Rashid Dostum, whose concept of "Let's roll" involves punishing his own soldiers by "tying them to tank tracks and then driving the tanks around his barracks' square to turn them into mincemeat."[4] Bush needed to evoke a masculine discourse to continue support for our bombing, to justify our actions, and to reinstate our heroism. This is just one of the many masculine phrases used to construct discourses on war—be strong, stand tall, protect our country, freedom, and way of life, never surrender—all these promote a vision of masculinity wherein the battle between countries is justified, glorified, and made intelligible. As such it becomes necessary to evoke the enemy as something wholly other than ourselves—as evil, insane, or cowardly, all of which have been used to describe Osama bin Laden (see "Evil"). However, if we explore the history of the United States we are often not the great hero defending the downtrodden, but are more often the bully defending our turf. We have supported leaders who have used state-sponsored terrorism to "disappear," torture, and kill thousands of dissidents in their own countries. The victims were most often the poor and downtrodden. The United States and its conflicts with others have often been saturated with masculinist discourse and have been fraught with contradiction.

The discourse of the coward seems to be working. However, it is not seamless in its function—an opinion poll aired on CNN on November 11, 2001 showed that only 56 percent of Americans supported our continued war in Afghanistan if it were to last more than five years; this statistic, however, was not discussed.[5] Although George W. Bush and Donald Rumsfeld say that the war on terrorism "will take a long time," the poll shows that the U.S. support for the long haul may be waning. Yet domestic dissent, such as protests in New York City and San Francisco, is rarely shown in the media. Mainstream media and governmental discourses represent the hero still having full support in his effort to bring the coward to justice. The cowardice of bin Laden and the Taliban must be reiterated, because without a coward there is no hero. We need to question their masculinity in order to reinstate and perpetuate our own. We can only see them as cowards, or a more complex picture could emerge, one that would make the bully all too evident.

Could the men who bombed New York and Washington, D.C., on 9/11 be considered anything other than cowards? Could there be a representation that, while not making their actions acceptable, engages in a more complex analysis? Can we handle nonbinary thinking? If a more complex analysis is offered, does it automatically become justification, as opposed to making sense of how it could be that men could take their own lives and the lives of so many others? In the rest of this essay, I will attempt to offer a more complex analysis, one that tries to move beyond the binaries of hero/coward to make sense the actions of nineteen men on 9/11. A sociological examination of suicide will provide a more complex analysis of an event that until now has only been defined as cowardly and evil in the discourses constructed by the media and U.S. government.

Suicide is often constructed in popular discourses as one of two things: (1) brave, as in giving one's life for one's country, or (2) cowardly, as taking the easy way out and not really dealing with the difficulties of life. The bombers of 9/11 and their suicides have been constructed as cowardly by the Western media. Emile Durkheim, an early French sociologist, theorizes that suicide, far from being an individual illness, is directly related to the particular social and cultural context in which an individual lives.[6] Therefore, suicide is not a binary between bravery and cowardice but an act determined by dynamic social forces. The psychology of the individual therefore is not the determining factor for acts of suicide; rather, an individual's society helps determine the range of possible actions. Durkheim theorizes four different types of suicide: egoistic, anomic, fatalistic, and altruistic. Egoistic suicide is the result of a society that promotes extreme individualism, one in which there is little connection between the individual and his or her community. Anomic suicide is a function of the rapid social shift that occurs when a society changes its norms and values. When this happens, people cannot make sense of the new societal rules, norms, or values and feel lost and confused about the world around them. Fatalistic suicide is a result of an oppressive situation. In other words, people will be more likely to take their own lives when they are living in a situation where there is little to no hope of alleviating the oppressive conditions under which they live. Lastly, altruistic suicide is the result of an extremely tight-knit society wherein the rules or values guiding the society are so strong that the values of the collective group become more important than the life of the individual. In this case, the individual takes his or her life for a society and a belief system that is larger and more important than the self of the individual.

The men who hijacked the planes on 9/11 were not cowards, but rather fit into one or more of the categories of suicide discussed above.[7] To flatten their actions into cowardice ignores the social differences and social forces in which each of them lived. Some of the factors may have been fatalistic, while others might have been altruistic and others egoistic or anomic. Since their histories, nationalities, and personalities differed, it is highly problematic to describe all their actions in one manner. It is far more beneficial to examine their actions with regard to Durkheim's categories because in so doing, we can take into account social forces and their histories in a global context as opposed to solely individual psychology. If governmental and media discourses were to explore 9/11 in this manner, it would force them to reevaluate their strategies. Their discourses would have to move beyond binaries and could not simply perpetuate the belief that violent acts carried out in our name are heroic, while constructing the violent acts of others as cowardly. Changing the discourse in this manner opens up the possibility of legitimate dialogue as opposed to military aggression founded on the language of hypermasculinity.

Whenever an act of so-called terrorism occurs, it immediately gets constructed as cowardly. We will hear this construction again, whether it is from the U.S. Senate describing the "faceless cowards"; from the mayor of New York City showing the "cowardly terrorists that they're not going to make us afraid"; from the Senate Majority leader opening the "doors of democracy" in the "face of such cowardly and heinous acts"; or from the average citizen with no words to describe "those responsible for Tuesday's acts" except "deranged and hopeless cowards." However, we must work to hear beyond the masculine constructions of these events, to incorporate a wider conception of what motivates them and how to address them. Far more than our masculinity is at stake, and we may end up losing everything in an attempt to protect that masculinity.

**NOTES**

1. The *Globe* is a tabloid paper which took a break from its exposés on Hollywood stars to conduct exposés of both Osama bin Laden and the attack of 9/11. In their coverage of the conflict readers saw something very similar to tabloid stories on the 1991 Persian Gulf War: "a version of war that was sometimes silly or incredible but always supportive of the U.S. military intervention." Tabloids sensationalize the war, its hero, and its villains

to provide a comedic, but also patriotic discourse of cowardice. See L. Rifas, "Supermarket Tabloids and Persian Gulf Dissent," in S. Jeffords and L. Rabinovitz, *Seeing through the Media: The Persian Gulf War* (New Brunswick: Rutgers University Press, 1994), 229.

2. For more on the ways in which media discourses construct Arab masculinity and particularly their constructions of Saddam Hussein, which is similar to the current constructions of bin Laden, see Anne Norton, "Gender, Sexuality and the Iraq of Our Imagination," *Middle East Report* (1991): 26–28.

3. George Lakoff, "Metaphor and War: The Metaphor System Used to Justify War in the Gulf," *Vietnam Generation Journal and Newsletter*, vol. 3, no. 3 (1991).

4. Robert Fisk, "What will the Northern Alliance do in our name now? I dread to think. . . . 'Why do we always have this ambiguous, dangerous relationship with our allies?'" *Independent*, November 14, 2001.

5. "Americans seem committed to winning war on terrorism." November 12, 2001 (www.gallup.com/poll/releases).

6. Emile Durkheim, *Suicide: A Study of Sociology* (London: Routledge, 1952).

7. Lamis Andoni, in an article on suicide bombings amongst Palestinian youth, theorizes that it is desperation, hopelessness, continual social flux, and religion that influenced two young Palestinians to take their lives in suicide missions against Israeli soldiers in 1996. It is clear that fatalism, anomie, and altruism were present in the culture in which these men lived and directly affected the decision to take their own life. See Lamis Andoni, "Searching for Answers: Gaza's Suicide Bombers," *Journal of Palestine Studies*, vol. 26, no. 4 (1997): 33–45.

**SUGGESTIONS FOR FURTHER READING**

Jeffords, Susan, and Lauren Rabinovitz, eds. *Seeing through the Media: The Persian Gulf War*. New Brunswick: Rutgers University Press, 1994.

McClintock, Anne. *Imperial Leather: Race, Gender, and Sexuality in the Colonial Conquest*. New York: Routledge, 1995.

Theweleit, Klaus. *Male Fantasies, Volume 1: Women, Floods, Bodies, History*. Minneapolis: University of Minnesota Press, 1987.

"Gulpin' gargoyles, Harry, people are still scared. Blimey, this is difficult. See, there was this wizard who went...bad. As bad as you could go. Worse. Worse than worse. His name was...*Voldemort*. Don' make me say it again. Anyway, this – this wizard, about twenty years ago now, started lookin' fer followers. Got 'em, too – some were afraid, some just wanted a bit o' his power, 'cause he was gettin' himself power, all right. Dark days, Harry."

"THIS IS A NEW KIND OF EVIL, AND WE UNDERSTAND, AND THE AMERICAN PEOPLE ARE BEGINNING TO UNDERSTAND, THIS CRUSADE, THIS WAR ON TERRORISM, IS GOING TO TAKE A WHILE, AND THE AMERICAN PEOPLE MUST BE PATIENT. . . . WE WILL RID THE WORLD OF THE EVILDOERS. THEY HAVE ROUSED A MIGHTY GIANT, AND MAKE NO MISTAKE ABOUT IT, WE'RE DETERMINED."

Zone 4, *Evil. Reprinted with the permission of Zone 4.*

# 5. Evil

LAURA J. REDIEHS

The concept of "evil" contains ambiguities and evokes fear. By employing the term "evil," social institutions generate fear to manipulate people's attitudes and behaviors. One theory about "evil" is especially powerful for summoning support for violent or militaristic action. As evidenced by both the September 11 attacks and the U.S. responses to those attacks, evil can be a powerful tool in the hands of political leaders. Under a different theory, however, a violent or militaristic response is thought to be incapable of solving the real problems that underlie actions or events regarded as evil.

There are several ways to define "good" and "evil," and some people even question the very existence of evil or the usefulness of the concept of evil. For the purpose of this essay, rather than questioning the existence of evil, I would like to focus on one important ambivalence in discussions about evil. This ambivalence results from two very different ways in which the reality of evil might be acknowledged. According to one theory, evil is an irrational force that inheres in people. According to the other theory, there is no irrational force of evil as such. Rather, the kinds of actions or events that get called evil arise from a complex of psychological, relational, and social-structural factors that ultimately could be identified and correctively transformed. In the first theory, which could be called the *individual theory*, evil is a force or principle residing in human beings. There are variations on this theme, from the view that there is evil mixed with goodness in all people, to the view that only some people contain evil, to the view that there are even some people, and perhaps entire groups of people, who are entirely evil. What brings all these views together under one theory is the core belief that evil is internal to the individual.

In the second theory, which could be called the *structural theory*, the word "evil" should properly only be applied to specific actions or events. While it is usually acknowledged that it is primarily events arising out of human choices and actions that are regarded as evil, those people responsible are not regarded as evil themselves. Instead, the people who brought forth evil are thought to have done so either because they mistakenly thought they were doing something good, or because they mistakenly felt justified in inflicting harm. The origin of evil, then, is not an evil principle within people; instead, evil is regarded as arising when people make significant errors of judgment that result from their reaching their intellectual or psychological limits; that is, when people make decisions without enough information (or from faulty information) or when people are severely stressed or feel very hurt or fearful, they can make serious mistakes. Under this second theory of evil, all actions that are regarded as evil can be traced back to these kinds of causes.

Both theories of evil, of course, assume that it is possible to identify "evil" in some objective sense. In addition, each theory suggests a different response to evil. In both cases, when evil is done, it demands a response. Both theories call for the elimination of evil. But how to go about eliminating evil varies depending on the theory of evil. On the evil-force theory, since evil inheres in people, the strategy is to find the people responsible for bringing forth the evil, and either kill them or restrain them from bringing forth further evil. On the structural theory of evil, there is no clear distinction between good people and evil people, and therefore the strategy of finding and eliminating specific people is considered not really to address the actual problem. The strategy suggested by the structural theory, then, is more complex. Diagnosing the origins and operations of human evil requires careful consideration of the psychological and conceptual states of the people involved in the situation, and of the way these states are influenced by the wider social systems in which people are embedded. The successful solution to the problem is identifying the conditions that led to the emergence of the evil outcomes, and then transforming those conditions so that the dynamic out of which evil emerged does not repeat itself.

Because the structural theory recommends a strategy that is more complex and difficult, the individual theory may seem more attractive and useful. It is less intellectually complex and demanding. It is psychologically more appealing, because in regarding ourselves as "good" and the ones whose actions we dislike as "evil," we can feel comforted by our own sense of moral superiority and do not have to go through the painful work of examining our own consciences and dealing with guilt, sorrow, or remorse. Nor do we have to engage in the difficult process of trying to understand and communicate with people we hate or fear. And finally, we do not have to take on the extremely difficult work of trying to change others and perhaps also ourselves in order to resolve the situation. It is far easier for all of us to resist change and simply try to destroy those we don't like. In fact, this attitude is the very origin of violence: violence is the impulse to close out, push out, or destroy those whom we regard as a threat to our own sense of comfort, goodness, or well-being.

When the events of September 11 unfolded, many people felt that they were witnessing evil. In the anger, fear, and sorrow that they felt, many wanted the comfort and clarity of the evil-force theory: there were evil people who were responsible, and if we could just find them and kill them, the world would be safe again and life could return to normal. This theory of evil is in fact exactly the one that underlies the official U.S. position as presented by President Bush. The rhetoric of Bush's speeches and news conferences shows the construction of the kind of ideology of good versus evil that is meant to justify a violent, militaristic response. Furthermore, he employs clever rhetorical strategies that play on both our wishful thinking and our fears in order to persuade by emotion rather than logic. After showing how this first theory of evil emerges out of his speeches, we will consider how useful and self-consistent this theory (and its attendant strategy) actually is.

First of all, examine how he explains why we were targeted for attack: "America was targeted for attack because we're the brightest beacon for freedom and opportunity in the world." In subsequent speeches, he adds to this list: they hate our democratically elected government; they hate our tolerance of openness and our creative culture. While it is possible that all this is true, the question of whether it is the full answer to the question of why we were attacked remains open. Such language makes "the enemy" seem monstrous and irrational, incomprehensibly hating what we regard as unquestionably good. No attempt is made to give them the benefit of the doubt, to consider that they might be misunderstanding us, might have felt hurt by something we had done, or might be afraid of us. Because we have been hurt, we want them to be evil, irrational monsters who have hurt us—not ordinary human beings who of course could not help but notice how wonderful and good we are.

The language of evil thus reinforces the process of making the enemy look monstrous. In his speech on September 11, Bush described the terrible events of that day as evil, and tied evil into human nature. The idea of evil people was then made more explicit in later speeches. For example, in a news conference on October 11, Bush said, "I think it's essential that all moms and dads and citizens tell their children we love them and there is love in the world, but also remind them there are evil people." Specific evil people were then identified during this news conference: Osama bin Laden and Saddam Hussein.

Then more is done to show just how horrible the evil people are. They are trained in tactics of terror and are "sent to hide in countries around the world to plot evil and destruction." They are directed "to kill Christians and Jews, to kill all Americans and make no distinctions among military and civilians, including women and children." Not only do they kill, they do so with satisfaction: "We have seen the true nature of these terrorists in the nature of their attacks; they kill thousands of innocent people and then rejoice about it. They kill fellow Muslims, many of whom died in the World Trade Center that terrible morning, and then they gloat. They condone murder and claim to be doing so in the name of a peaceful religion." But: "We're not deceived by their pretenses to piety."

And it is not just the terrorists themselves at fault. Others as well become guilty by association: "By aiding and abetting murder, the Taliban regime is committing murder." Several of Bush's speeches contained long lists of the additional evils endorsed by the Taliban: from stealing food intended for starving people to forbidding children to fly kites or build snowmen. Completing the picture of just how despicable "the enemy" is: "We hunt an enemy that hides in shadows and caves" (see "Cowardice").

Because the enemy is so clearly evil, a military response is required. This connection was made explicit when Bush spoke with reporters at the White House following his November 6 satellite speech to a summit in Warsaw, Poland. Referring again to bin Laden, Bush said, "This is an evil man that we're dealing with, and I wouldn't put it past him to develop evil weapons to try to harm civilization as we know it. That's why we work hard to keep our coalition bound together, and that's why we're going to keep relentless military pressure on him in Afghanistan." In an earlier speech, he spoke of directing "every resource at our command" to this task, claiming that "the only way to defeat terrorism as a threat to our way of life is to stop it, eliminate it and destroy it where it grows." The response is thus one of vengeance and violence, expressed in unambiguous terms of elimination and destruction.

But this may take a while, as the goal is an ambitious one: this war "will not end until every terrorist group of global reach has been found, stopped and defeated." Stating the goal this way is disturbing, as the very impossibility of determining whether we have actually succeeded suggests that we may be living fearfully and in this state of war not just for a long time, but forever. How can we ever be sure we have found every terrorist group? What exactly would it take to permanently stop and defeat them? The image is made even more horrifying by statements such as this one from the same speech: "Our response involves far more than instant retaliation and isolated strikes. Americans should not expect one battle, but a lengthy campaign unlike any other we have ever seen." The vagueness of what is meant by "lengthy campaign" (something *more than* retaliation and military strikes) is also cause for alarm.

This characterization of the enemy as wholly evil is then further reinforced by language that draws sharp lines between only two sides, good versus evil. This event is part of a great cosmic battle: "This will be a monumental struggle of good versus evil. But good will prevail." More specifically, it is freedom and fear that are at war. Therefore, the advance of human freedom "now depends on us. Our nation, this generation, will lift the dark threat of violence from our people and our future." With this language,

Bush appeals to our noble sentiments in order to solicit our support for his strategy: we find ourselves playing a crucial role during a decisive moment in the Great Cosmic Battle between Good and Evil.

Hence, people and countries must choose which side they are on: "Every nation in every region now has a decision to make. Either you are with us or you are with the terrorists. From this day forward, any nation that continues to harbor or support terrorism will be regarded by the United States as a hostile regime." Such sharp polarization between people and groups who are good and those who are bad again shows that Bush subscribes to the theory that evil inheres in people. The sharp division also supports a sharp division in possible responses: if you are on the side of "goodness," you have no choice but to support the military actions of the United States. No other response is adequate: "I will put every nation on notice that these duties involve more than sympathy or words. No nation can be neutral in this conflict because no civilized nation can be secure in a world threatened by terrorism."

Yet there is the problem that, at first glance, the violence of our own response may make us look as evil as the terrorists. But since we are good, even if our actions may sometimes look as horrific as those of the enemy, they are, in fact, justified. Our military campaign and the war against terror is "making good progress in a just cause," and Bush emphasizes that "we are not targeting civilians" (see "Justice" and "Targets"). Responding to words of caution such as those expressed by Algerian President Abdelaziz Bouteflika that the military operation in Afghanistan must minimize civilian deaths, Bush said, "Our efforts are directed at terrorists and military targets, because unlike our enemies, we value human life." This sentiment is echoed in Bush's speech to the United Nations: "Unlike the enemy, we seek to minimize—not maximize—the loss of innocent life."

So, although both sides in this Great Cosmic Battle employ similar techniques—violence that includes the killing of innocent civilians—*our* doing this is justified because we are good; *their* doing this is unjustified because they are evil. What then does the distinction of good versus evil depend on, if not the actual killing of innocent people? The rhetoric itself gives the answer: we value human life; we don't intend to kill civilians; in fact we minimize rather than maximize the loss of innocent life (suggesting that we are aware that military action inevitably results in the loss of innocent life), whereas they, the evil enemies, *intend* to kill lots of innocent people and then gloat when they succeed. What differentiates the good people, then, from the evil ones is a difference of feelings and attitudes. In this picture of good versus evil, all that is required to maintain goodness is to *not intend* to kill innocent people, and to *feel remorse* if one happens to have done so. What makes the deaths of innocent people bad, then, is not their actual deaths, but the attitudes and feelings of those who killed them. Therefore, it is easy to justify actions that lead to the loss of innocent lives: such actions are justified if the people responsible for those actions have the right *feelings*.

There are two problems with this theory of justification. The first is that it is all too easy for us to *say* that we have the right kinds of feelings, and the enemies have the wrong kinds of feelings, and so we are good and they are evil. But how do we really *know* the feelings, attitudes, and intentions of others? If we were wrong about their feelings and attitudes, and in fact they do regard some people as innocent, do not wish to harm those people, and feel bad if their actions do result in the loss of these lives, then are the enemies, in fact, good after all? And are all their actions therefore justified, just as the violence we engage in is justified?

The second problem with this theory of evil concerns the sincerity and rationality of the attitudes of our leaders. They claim to regret the loss of innocent lives, and they claim not to intend such loss. Yet they embark on military strategies that they know will result in the loss of innocent lives. (Note again Bush's comment that we seek to *minimize* the loss of innocent life—thus he admits that he knows that the loss of innocent life is inevitable. Otherwise, he would have said we seek to *eliminate* the loss of innocent life.) "Rationality" is usually defined as choosing a course of action that seems likely to bring about intended consequences. For people to claim not to intend a particular consequence (such as killing innocent people), and then to engage in actions that they know will result in that consequence is either disingenuous (they in fact do not care about the loss of innocent lives), or irrational.

Now we come to some other incongruities in Bush's speeches. In his speech to the United Nations on November 10, Bush claims that, "We choose the dignity of life over a culture of death. We choose lawful change and civil disagreement over coercion, subversion and chaos." And yet we are engaged in military action that is coercive and brings chaos to Afghanistan. Our leaders have not handled this lawfully by revealing the evidence that they have against those who have been accused of the atrocities of September 11, and then bringing those accused to some kind of fair trial. The incongruity is even clearer in the next few sentences of this speech: "These commitments—hope and order, law and life—unite people across cultures and continents. Upon these commitments depend all peace and progress. For these commitments we are determined to fight." While the concept of "fighting for peace" may be meaningful in a figurative way even though it is obviously self-contradictory taken literally, it is clear, under the circumstances, that Bush does not mean this figuratively since, in fact, we are literally fighting in a war. Finally, also in the same speech, Bush says: "Peace will only come when all have sworn off forever incitement, violence and terror." If peace can *only* come through swearing off violence, what justifies our participation in violence? Would it not make more sense for the United States to be a true leader and to be the first to swear off violence, seeking instead other ways of addressing this conflict?

Having seen how Bush tries to construct a rationale for military action on the basis of the first theory of evil, we must now pause to consider the question of which theory of evil, the evil-force theory or the structural theory, is the correct one. Does evil arise from an evil principle (an irrational hatred of what is good) that acts through some people, or does evil arise from some combination of misunderstanding and psychological stress? How does one even begin to answer a question like this?

Before trying to answer this question, there are a couple of points worth noting. First, since the different theories suggest different strategies of response, the answer to the question of which theory is right really matters. If we choose the wrong theory, our response is not likely to be effective. Second, it is also important to note that a careful investigation into the answer to the question of which theory is correct *is* to embark on the strategy suggested by the structural theory—it is to look more closely into human nature in quest of understanding. To accept the evil-force theory instead, without careful investigation into who was actually responsible for the horrible deeds in question and what their motivations really were, is simply to make up a story about what one wants to believe rather than facing reality.

Absent the necessary empirical investigation that would prove one theory or the other to be true, are there other good reasons to support one of the theories over the other? One of the problems with the evil-force theory started to emerge toward the end of the analysis of Bush's speeches: the incongruities in his statements suggest that perhaps this theory is not consistent. Fanning the flames of fear in order to solicit support for a war *against* fear, invoking violence to bring about a peace that cannot be found until everyone swears off violence, and defining evil in terms of the loss of innocent lives while justifying a militaristic response that is admitted also to involve the loss of innocent lives are three examples of the problematic inconsistencies.

Another problem with the evil-force theory is that it is very simple when reality usually turns out to be more complex. Furthermore, as was pointed out earlier in this essay, this theory is psychologically appealing, making us feel good about ourselves and saving us the hard work of being respectful toward those who hurt us, frighten us, think us bad, or are difficult to understand. It is precisely this appealing dimension of the evil-force theory that should make us suspicious of its truth. It is *too* easy. It is in fact so easy that it reeks of delusory wishful thinking. In our individual lives, most of us tend to grow beyond literally fighting over our differences and learn to talk them through instead. Furthermore, most of us tend to grow beyond thinking that particular people are clearly good or bad, and come to appreciate that people are more complicated than that—that everyone is capable of doing good or harm; that everyone, when asked, generally *feels* justified in doing what they do (or apologizes when they come to realize that they have done harm); and that the reasons that people sometimes do bad things are complex. If we can work well with these complex understandings of each other as adults within society, why can't societies, organizations, countries, and governments apply analogous patterns of thought and strategies of response at the level of international disagreements and conflicts?

As a final reflection on the two theories of evil, let us consider a very plausible scenario. Imagine that the structural theory is true, but we adopt the strategy of the individual theory instead. Attempting to eliminate the evil by killing the evil people (or otherwise disempowering them) would not actually address the problem of evil. Instead, it would leave the conditions that produced the evil in place, and might in fact produce more harmful acts in the future; the cycle of violence would continue. Clearly the only potentially effective option in such a situation would be to identify and transform the systems that created the conditions in which the evil actions took place. This example suggests that whatever "evil" actually is, the structural strategy is more rational and useful, for evil cannot really be eliminated through violence. Consequently, rhetorical strategies of trying to justify violence by invoking the language of evil are highly problematic. The inconsistencies in the individual theory explain why employing this strategy perpetuates the very violence that it claims to want to eliminate. It can be argued that the structural theory of evil is not properly a theory of evil at all: since no active principle of evil is postulated, every use of the word "evil" can be translated into a set of explainable factors, or a set of problems solvable by means other than violence. Indeed, good arguments can be made for avoiding the word "evil" altogether, since it tends to evoke the idea of an active, irrational force. We do not actually need this word in order to speak about what is terrible about terrible events, or to discuss possible responses to people who engage in actions that are harmful.

The danger of the very use of the language of evil is that the concept of evil is very powerful because of its capacity to evoke fear. Evoking fear, in turn, can be a very effective technique for social control (see "Anthrax"). Fear focuses attention on a very narrow range—solely upon perceived threats—and therefore can be used as a clever diversionary tactic. Fear also stirs up strong emotions, especially the overwhelming desire for security and strong impulses to separate oneself from perceived threats (with these impulses then generating hatred or the desire for revenge or other violent action). Because of this power behind the concept of evil, it is important to critically identify three rhetorical techniques employed in President Bush's speeches. The first two have already been questioned here: (1) his use of the rhetoric of evil to generate fear, manipulate public opinion, and generate popular support; and (2) his use of a particular interpretation of evil to create the impression that a violent, military intervention is the *only* viable response.

The third, and possibly the most worrisome technique is that Bush uses the rhetoric of evil to forcefully silence dissent. Not only is a sharp line drawn between good and evil, but the two sides of this dichotomy are filled out in a particular, strategic way, both with specific sets of concepts and with specific types or groups of people. On the side of goodness are the concepts of freedom, democracy, creativity, a "way of life," and "civilization," all necessarily to be defended with something "more" than mere words. On the side of evil are images of murderers lurking in caves, and women and children being beaten because of their socks, shoes, kites, and snowmen. Neutrality is not an option. There is no space for it in such a sharp dichotomy. Every attitude, action, or person must be assigned to one side or the other. Therefore, to question the official interpretation of these events, or to question the appropriateness of a military response, is to remove oneself from the side of goodness, because in a tightly dichotomized world, to question any part of one side of the divide is to question everything else associated with it. Therefore, the questioner must be regarded as evil, because there are no other ways of classifying someone who, by questioning some of what Bush has defined as good, is thereby questioning goodness itself!

It is crucial to recognize that this strategy of constructing a tight dichotomy of good versus evil is not a humble expression of a theory about reality, but is a power move. Bush's claim that "words are not enough" may be a clever masquerade for hiding the fact that he himself is powerfully wielding words to manipulate public thought and action. We must always keep in mind that *we* are in control of our words and concepts: we don't have to let words and concepts control us. When we do place ourselves at the mercy of words and concepts, we are placing ourselves at the mercy of the people who use those words and concepts to control us. The real way to preserve freedom and all the other noble ideals that Bush claims he is defending is to preserve our power to question how others use words and put thought into action. The only way to build lasting peace is to invoke the power of words in order to seek mutual understanding and reconcile our differences.

### SUGGESTIONS FOR FURTHER READING

Ansbro, John J., and Martin Luther King, Jr. *Nonviolent Strategies and Tactics for Social Change*. Lanham, Md.: Madison Books, Distributed by National Book Network, 1982.

Gandhi, M. K. *Non-Violent Resistance (Satyagraha)*. Mineola, N.Y.: Dover Publications, 1961.

Tolstoy, Leo. *The Kingdom of God Is Within You*. Translated by Constance Garnett. Lincoln: University of Nebraska Press, 1984.

Ury, William. *Getting to Peace: Transforming Conflict at Home, at Work, and in the World*. New York: Viking, 1999.

Wink, Walter, ed. *Peace Is the Way: Writings on Nonviolence from the Fellowship of Reconciliation*. Maryknoll, N.Y.: Orbis Books, 2000.

# 6. Freedom

Andrew D. Van Alstyne

In a September 20 address to a joint session of Congress, President Bush declared, "Tonight we are a country awakened to danger and called to defend freedom." In the course of the forty-one-minute applause-filled speech, the president used the terms "free" or "freedom" thirteen times. Although he frequently intoned the mantra of freedom, it was as a vague rhetorical device, rather than a substantive exploration of what it actually means. By making freedom sufficiently amorphous, Bush ignored the most democratically important meanings of freedom (e.g., a free press, freedom of assembly) and instead used the term as a device supporting policies that further a conservative agenda. Three primary policies Bush has pursued are the restriction of civil liberties, the expansion of free trade, and the freeing of the nation from foreign energy dependence. Examining the historical and economic context of these policies allows us to see that Bush's rhetoric of freedom not only generates support for the "war on terrorism" but also permits the continuation of U.S.–dominated economic globalization.

## The Treadmill of Production

In the wake of World War II, the United States emerged as the hegemonic nation within the global political economy. The dominant logic of this political economy can be metaphorically described as a "treadmill of production."[1] Understanding the logic of the treadmill helps to explain the U.S. government's current amorphous use of the word freedom. The treadmill of production describes the cumulative impact of several interrelated processes. Individual economic agents operating within a capitalist system are driven toward profit maximization and economic growth. Increasing withdrawals from and additions to the natural environment fuel the increasing economic growth, resulting in increased environmental strain. At the same time, checks on the cost of production maximize profit margins.

Two primary avenues to "efficiency" are: lower labor costs and increased use of technology. This results in increased social costs as the treadmill is "accelerated." The nonstatic nature of the treadmill provides for a form of political, social, and economic inertia. The more the treadmill accelerates, the more it becomes entrenched, the more it becomes the solution to the problems it creates. The metaphor of the treadmill fundamentally concerns itself with issues of production. Within our pluralist system, the logic of the treadmill spans the mainstream political spectrum. Indeed, challengers who mount serious opposition to the treadmill face severe consequences.

## Freedom from Freedom

Historically, in times of war, patriotism and national security have both been used to justify the widespread repression of civil liberties. During World War I, in order to stifle opposition to the war, the United States passed the Espionage Act, which forbade fomenting disloyalty among U.S. military forces or obstructing enlistment procedures. During World War II, the U.S. government set up concentration camps for over 110,000 people of Japanese descent; three-fourths of those interned were American citizens. Within these prison camps, people suffered for three years for no reason other than their ethnicity.

From the 1950s through the 1970s American political culture spawned a large number of social movements that fundamentally changed American society. These included movements for civil rights, free speech, women's rights, black power, American Indian rights, and environmental justice. All these, when combined with protests against the Vietnam War, sparked unprecedented domestic dissent. In order to contain the growing challenges to the political and economic status quo, the FBI launched a counterintelligence program, known as COINTELPRO, which officially lasted from 1956 through 1971. Its tactics included infiltration, disruption, and surveillance in an effort to discredit and neutralize these emerging movements. In addition, members of the black liberation movement faced severe coercive repression, including the widespread use of political assassination.

Social and political critics often use the term "Orwellian" to describe government policies that involve elements of government surveillance. The current moves to restrict freedoms in order to "protect" freedom, however, go beyond anything envisioned in Orwell's *1984*. On October 26, President Bush signed into law the Uniting and Strengthening America by Providing Appropriate Tools Required to Intercept and Obstruct Terrorism (USA PATRIOT) Act. Once again, the government has used patriotic fervor to garner widespread support for legislation: only one senator voted against the Act. According to Laura Murphy of the American Civil Liberties Union, "This bill goes light years beyond what is necessary to combat terrorism. Included in this bill are provisions that would allow for the mistreatment of immigrants, the suppression of dissent and the investigation and surveillance of wholly innocent Americans."[2] Social and political freedom in the United States stems directly from the separation of powers outlined in the Constitution. The USA PATRIOT Act diminishes the role of judicial oversight in criminal investigations as well as citizens' privacy. Key provisions of the Act include authorizing the police to perform search and seizure operations without informing suspects, opening the private records of suspected terrorists to investigators without the need for a court order, and allowing the FBI and CIA to share information collected in grand jury investigations. Proponents legitimize the bill by pointing out sunset provisions that expire in five years. However, not all aspects of the bill fall under the sunset clause, including the domestic empowerment of the CIA. Also, investigations that are under way prior to the expiration date may continue to use the expanded powers. While individuals' freedoms are decreasing, agents of repression now enjoy increased freedom from oversight.

Another step taken in the domestic war against terrorism involves the racial profiling of people who are potential terrorists based solely upon their race and ethnicity. The investigation into the attacks has led to the detention of nearly one thousand people so far. Most of the people in custody are being held on immigration violations or charges unrelated to terrorism. Allegations of police abuse have also surfaced.[3] In spite of President Bush's assertion, "The enemy of America is not our many Muslim friends; it is not our many Arab friends," coverage of racial profiling has been systematically uncritical.

## Free Trade

Following World War II, U.S. foreign policy coupled with the emerging international financial institutions (IFIs)—like the

World Bank and International Monetary Fund (IMF)—pursued geographical expansion and acceleration of the treadmill of production. Development projects of the World Bank in the 1950s and 1960s, structural adjustment programs (SAPs) in the late 1970s and 1980s, and current developmental goals of both the IMF and World Bank all seek to integrate Southern nations into the treadmill. The spread of multilateral trade agreements—the North American Free Trade Agreement (NAFTA) went into effect in 1994 and negotiations for a Free Trade Area of the Americas (FTAA) are ongoing—pursue similar treadmill logic. The World Trade Organization (WTO) coordinates the reduction of trade barriers in an attempt to foster increased trade, thus further following the dictates of the treadmill.

In a statement released on November 3, Osama bin Laden declared, "This war is fundamentally religious."[4] Yet the September 11 attacks did not target any form of institutionalized religion in the United States. Instead, one of the targets was the World Trade Center, which symbolized the global treadmill of production. Osama bin Laden confirmed this in an interview: "The 11 September attacks were not targeted at women and children. The real targets were America's icons of military and economic power."[5] In response to this challenge to the treadmill, President Bush reiterated the continued dominance of the treadmill's expansionary logic. In an October 24 address, he argued, "We fight a war at home; and part of the war we fight is to make sure that our economy continues to grow." Clearly, continued expansion of the treadmill, in the face of a substantive challenge, remains part of American policy.

Prior to the September 11 attacks, one of the administration's primary goals was fast-track negotiating status, the current incarnation of which is officially known as trade promotion authority. Fast track allows the president to negotiate trade treaties that are then presented to the Congress for a straight yes or no vote. Critics argue that fast track fundamentally goes against the traditional pluralist values of the United States. The 1998 congressional rejection of fast track provided a major victory for the opponents of corporate-centered globalization. A sustained struggle on the part of labor unions, environmental groups, as well as some conservative Republicans has helped to keep fast track from becoming a reality for President Bush. In the wake of September 11, fast track has remained a major priority of the administration. The emergence of fast track reflects Bush's own desire to be free—free from political restraint. On October 26, the president decreed,

> We can restore economic confidence by expanding trade. More open trade is essential to the growth of our nation's economy. A part of our economic recovery program is to give me the ability to negotiate trade agreements. I need trade promotion authority to expand opportunity, for businesses large and small, for entrepreneurs in America. I need trade promotion authority to expand the job base of this great nation. I'm the first President who hasn't had trade promotion authority. I need it now. It's in our nation's best interest that we have it. *And it's in the best interests of our world that we trade in freedom.* (emphasis added)

It would be difficult to find a clearer illustration of the treadmill's dominance. The president has not changed the substance of his political goals, in this case expansion of free trade. The rhetoric has undergone a significant transition, though. Defending the United States against terrorism is now equated with the expansion of free trade, which is now also known as the "trade in freedom."

On October 31, the president implicitly challenged the patriotism of those opposed to fast track, stating, "I'm confident in America's ability to compete. . . . I want to make it easier for the world to trade in freedom. . . . I know it's good for the spread of

American values if we trade freely around the world." This ignores the empirical reality that free trade is not free. In addition to the repression of civil liberties outlined above, the expansion of neoliberal economic policies restricts global citizen workers' freedom to participate in alternative political, social, and economic arrangements. Moreover, supposedly "free" trade has significant costs for ordinary people in terms of jobs, income, and environmental safety. Not content to allow his audience to make the connection between fast track opponents and a lack of faith in America, Bush continued: "I ask the Congress to be confident as we approach these big issues; be confident in the ability of the American people; be confident in the ability of the entrepreneur to succeed; be confident in our future." Opponents of fast track face the potential epithet of being "antipatriotic" for questioning the president's desire for treadmill expansion.

U.S. Trade Representative Robert Zoellick, whom Bush described as "traveling the world promoting free trade," explicitly illuminated the economic nature of the "war on terrorism." In a September 24 speech, Zoellick declared:

> Today's enemies will learn that America is the economic engine for freedom, opportunity, and development. Economic strength—at home and abroad—is the foundation of America's hard and soft power. To that end, U.S. leadership in promoting the international and economic and trading system is vital. Trade is about more than economic efficiency. *It promotes the values at the heart of this protracted struggle.*[6]

Generally, further acceleration of the treadmill is seen as the solution to strains created by the treadmill's actions. Zoellick's comments reinforce the power elite's commitment to the logic of the treadmill.

## Freedom from Foreign Energy Dependence

Another front in the battle against terrorism is a reduction in our
dependence on foreign oil supplies. Like the expansion of free
trade, the quest for energy stability has been an integral part of
recent American history. Among the myriad factors accounting
for the economic dominance of the United States following
World War II was the nation's indisputable edge in manufacturing. The expansion of the manufacturing sector, following the
logic of the treadmill of production, required increasing
amounts of energy input. While the United States tried to produce some of this energy domestically—via newly discovered
means of harnessing atomic fission—with horrendous social and
environmental results, the nation also turned to foreign oil
sources. The potential political instability of oil-producing nations such as Iran and Iraq, however, worried U.S. policy makers.

In 1951, Iran elected Mohammed Mossadegh prime minister.[7]
This represented a break from Iran's authoritarian tradition and
a potential move toward a U.S.–style liberal democracy.
Mossadegh's attempts to nationalize the oil industry angered
Northern nations that were becoming increasingly dependent
upon oil exports from the Middle East. In response, the CIA col-
laborated with the British Secret Service on a plan to overthrow
Mossadegh and replace him with a government that would insure uninterrupted oil supplies. In 1953, the CIA put into operation a mission that ultimately ended Mossadegh's prime minis-
tership and consolidated the power of the Shah, who would rule
until 1979, using his secret police to stamp out dissent and maintain his grip on power. The overthrow of Mossadegh thus demonstrates the relative American priority of oil over democracy.

The Iranian coup clearly demonstrates the dominance of the
treadmill of production in the U.S. political economy. The political form of Iranian society, democracy, had taken steps toward

challenging the treadmill of production in two key ways. First, the nationalization of industry directly challenged the ability of corporations within the oil industry to profit from the extraction, refinement, and sale of oil. Second, direct control of oil by the Iranian government potentially threatened multinational corporations' need for stable energy supplies. Actions that could potentially challenge the treadmill are dealt with swiftly and surely—but with potentially negative long-term consequences for U.S. policy (see "Blowback").

Iraq's 1990 invasion and occupation of Kuwait inspired the same fear about oil supply disruption as Mossadegh's attempt at nationalization of the Iranian oil industry. During the Iran-Iraq war, the United States at times had aided Iraqi President Saddam Hussein, because of U.S. opposition to the Ayatollah Khomeini (who became Iran's leader after the overthrow of the Shah in 1979). In January 1991, the elder President Bush received congressional approval for military involvement in Kuwait. Although the United States had ignored or been involved in countless other examples of aggression—in Iran, Chile, Nicaragua, and East Timor, to name a few—the official purpose of the Gulf War was the liberation of Kuwait. American military involvement led to the expulsion of Iraq from Kuwait, but failed to remove Hussein from power. Indeed, the United States still frequently bombs Iraq and is also behind economic sanctions that are responsible for the deaths of over half a million children under the age of five.

American intervention in the Gulf War again demonstrates the degree of political support and defense of the treadmill of production. In order to safeguard stable access to oil, the United States waged a war in the name of "freedom." This conclusion is further reinforced when one considers that Kuwait was never a free country, in the sense of being democratic. Unfettered treadmill expansion trumped the strictly political logic of democracy.

In recent years, drilling for oil in the Arctic National Wildlife Refuge (ANWR) has been one of the most politically contentious environmental issues in the United States. During the 2000 presidential election campaign, it marked one of the most clear-cut differences between Al Gore, who opposed drilling, and George Bush, who supported drilling. The Bush energy plan, drafted by a secret committee led by Vice President Dick Cheney, called for opening ANWR to drilling. In August, the House of Representatives passed legislation allowing for exploration in ANWR; this legislation failed in the Senate. After September 11, pressure for drilling mounted. The spirit of bipartisan consensus that emerged following the September 11 attacks splintered over calls for drilling in ANWR. On October 17, President Bush reiterated his call for drilling in ANWR: "I ask Congress to now act on an energy bill that the House of Representatives passed back in August. . . . Too much of our energy comes from the Middle East. . . . Our country needs greater energy independence. This issue is a matter of national security, and I hope the Senate acts quickly." Again, driven by the logic of the treadmill, Bush took a policy initiative debated prior to September 11 and reframed it in terms of national security. This raises the political stakes for drilling opponents, by forcing them to "prove" their patriotism. However, Senate opponents to drilling have been able to navigate the fine line between dissent and a lack of patriotism. Senator Frank Murkowski introduced an amendment that would have opened the Arctic National Wildlife Refuge to drilling. Seeing the impending defeat, he joined with his fellow senators in defeating the amendment 99-0.

## Consent and Dissent

During the current war on terrorism, the mainstream media in the United States has presented a one-sided story, in effect being the "tail wagging the dog" of public support for the war. According to a memo written by CNN Chair Walter Isaacson and distributed to CNN reporters: "As we get good reports from Taliban-controlled Afghanistan, we must redouble our efforts to make sure we do not seem to be simply reporting from their vantage or perspective."[8] Nor are alternative viewpoints making it into mainstream newspapers: of forty-six op-ed pieces in the *New York Times* and *Washington Post* in the three weeks following the attacks, forty-four argued for a military response, while only two raised other possibilities.[9] Clearly, the media is playing an active role in "manufacturing consent" in favor of the war in all its manifestations.

Following September 11, pundits pronounced variations on the theme that "nothing will ever be the same." In concluding an examination of policies taken in the name of "freedom," this issue must be broached. In many ways, the conventional wisdom accurately describes the current state of affairs. From a social psychological viewpoint, the American populace clearly has seen a fundamental transition in its worldview. An attack of this scale against the home soil of Northern nations by agents of Southern nations is unprecedented. The American mind-set now faces fears of further attacks and so willingly goes along with a war whose stated purpose is a literal impossibility: the eradication of terrorism and evil.

Using the treadmill of production as a metaphor for understanding the contemporary political economy reveals a different picture. The policies that the government has proposed and/or implemented in the wake of September 11 represent a continuation of previous American trajectories. Perhaps the most fundamental change has come not in the policies themselves, but within the political climate in which those policies are enacted. Conflicts between different interest groups within the political economy shape the political economy. What September 11 has done is provide one side with ammunition (patriotism and the defense of freedom) that is nearly invincible, at least for the time being, while diminishing the political power of opposition groups.

As the overwhelming passage of the USA PATRIOT Act shows, there is little political space for dissent against the current move to restrict civil liberties. Trade promotion authority represents the administration's focus on the expansion of free trade. At this time, the status of fast track is in doubt. In the absence of a sufficient number of votes to insure passage, it is unlikely that it will be introduced into Congress. The attempt to gain access to oil reserves in the Arctic National Wildlife Refuge has proved to be the largest obstacle facing the Bush Administration.

All the issues discussed in this essay, as well as the war against Afghanistan, represent potential sources of legitimate political conflict. Unlike most other issues, there is a noticeable space for dissent when it comes to the environment. Potentially, this could be a stepping-stone to a broadened political dialogue eventually expanding to other issues discussed here. There seems to be a correlation between the direct relationship of an issue to security following September 11 and the amount of allowable dissent. Thus, the seemingly depoliticized role of the natural environment in the case of the Arctic National Wildlife Refuge could pave the way for further environmental action (for example, environmental justice issues surrounding air pollution caused by the attacks on the World Trade Center and the rescue workers still sifting through the rubble, who are breathing the air on a daily basis).

Also, the conceptual linkage between free trade and terrorism, while not as vague as that of the environment, is not as clear-cut as the repression of civil liberties. Thus, an expansion into this issue seems a viable option in the near future, sweeping in on the coattails of the environment. Creating spaces for politically viable dissent will allow the racist nature of the investigation into terrorism to be challenged. In the long run, the challenge for scholars and activists will be to link environmental exploitation to international inequality, domestic repression, and racism. The absence of such an analysis will reduce the potential creation of just social arrangements.

While amorphous definitions of freedom have fueled the trajectories outlined in this essay, redefining freedom could potentially empower dissenting voices. Instead of freedom to consume U.S. products and lifestyles, a definition of freedom focusing upon human rights is needed. Bush's political freedom, in part, has stemmed from wrapping himself in the vagueness of freedom and its centrality to the mainstream American ideology. Arguments that global citizens deserve freedom from racism, sexism, homophobia, disease, starvation, environmental degradation, and other forms of oppression challenge current trajectories of the U.S. and global political economy. The real work of freedom lies not in the waging of war, the unchecked depletion of resources, or the feeding of the treadmill's voracious appetite, but rather in combating these practices wherever and whenever they occur.

**NOTES**

1. See Allan Schnaiberg, *The Environment: From Surplus to Scarcity* (New York: Oxford University Press, 1980); Allan Schnaiberg and Kenneth Gould, *Environment and Society: The Enduring Conflict* (New York: St. Martin's Press, 1994); Kenneth Gould, Allan Schnaiberg, and Adam Weinberg, *Local Environmental Struggles: Citizen Activism in the Treadmill of Production*

(New York: Cambridge University Press, 1996); Adam Weinberg, David Pellow, and Allan Schnaiberg, *Urban Recycling and the Search for Sustainable Community Development* (Princeton: Princeton University Press, 2000).

2. Quoted in John Nichols, "Terror Law: A Win for Fear, a Loss for Freedom," *Nation* (2001) online (http://www.thenation.com/thebeat).

3. "N.Y. Detainees in Terrorist Attacks Allege Abuse" (November 3, 2001) (http://www.usatoday.com/news/attack/2001/10/30/detainees-treatment.htm).

4. Osama bin Laden (2001). The text of the statement is taken from the BBC (http://news.bbc.co.uk/hi/english/world/monitoring/media_reports/newsid_1636000/1636782.stm).

5. Interview with Osama bin Laden (November 11, 2001) (http://www.observer.co.uk/waronterrorism/story/0,1373,591508,00.html).

6. Emphasis added. Robert Zoellick, "American Trade Leadership: What Is at Stake" (September 24, 2001) (http://www.ustr.gov/speech-test/zoellick/zoellick_9.PDF).

7. The history of the Iranian coup is drawn from James Risen, "Secrets of History: The CIA in Iran," *New York Times* (2000) (http://www.nytimes.com/library/world/mideast/041600iran-cia-index.html).

8. Quoted in Fairness and Accuracy in Reporting (FAIR) "CNN Says Focus on Civilian Casualties Would Be 'Perverse'" (November 1, 2001) (http://www.fair.org/activism/cnn-casualties.html).

9. FAIR, "Op-Ed Echo Chamber: Little Space for Dissent to the Military Line" (November 2,2001) (http://www.fair.org/activism/nyt-wp-opeds.html).

## SUGGESTIONS FOR FURTHER READING

Blackstock, Nelson. *COINTELPRO: The FBI's Secret War on Political Freedom.* New York: Vintage Books, 1975.

Churchill, Ward, and Jim Vander Wall. *The COINTELPRO Papers: Documents from the FBI's Secret Wars against Dissent in the United States.* Boston: South End Press, 1990.

Gould, Kenneth, Allan Schnaiberg, and Adam Weinberg. *Local Environmental Struggles: Citizen Activism in the Treadmill of Production.* New York: Cambridge University Press, 1996.

Joppke, Christian. *Mobilizing against Nuclear Energy: A Comparison of Germany and the United States.* Berkeley: University of California Press, 1993.

Mills, C. Wright. *The Power Elite.* New York: Oxford University Press, 1956.

Schnaiberg, Allan. *The Environment: From Surplus to Scarcity.* New York: Oxford University Press, 1980.

Schnaiberg, Allan, and Kenneth Gould. *Environment and Society: The Enduring Conflict.* New York: St. Martin's Press, 1994.

Weinberg, Adam, David Pellow, and Allan Schnaiberg. *Urban Recycling and the Search for Sustainable Community Development.* Princeton: Princeton University Press, 2000.

# 7. Fundamentalism

LEAH RENOLD

We are at war, declares an article in the *New York Times* published shortly after the attacks on the World Trade Center.[1] The author, Andrew Sullivan, argues that we are in a religious war, a war that threatens our very existence. Not only our lives, but also our souls are at stake. Who is the enemy? It is not Islam. It is a specific form of Islam called fundamentalism. In his essay Sullivan argues that fundamentalism constitutes a large section of Islam. The article explains that fundamentalism has ancient roots and has attracted thousands of adherents for centuries from different religious faiths, including Christianity and Judaism.

Sullivan's essay in the *New York Times* is only one of many articles and broadcasts in the U.S. media since the attacks on the World Trade Center that use "fundamentalism" as a category to describe those groups targeted as enemies of the American people. The term has been applied to the political and religious positions of Osama bin Laden and the Taliban, as well as a significant portion of the world's Muslims. "Islamic fundamentalism" has been used so frequently in the media since September 11 that publishers of history textbooks are now scrambling to revise their books to include discussions of the term. An article in the *Wall Street Journal* reports that in a rush to update textbooks, Prentice Hall, the publisher of *The American Nation*, the top-selling

U.S. history textbook for middle-school students, has begun to highlight the topic of Islamic fundamentalism, where previously the topic had not been included.[2]

When the term "fundamentalist" is used in the media in association with Islam, it is rarely defined. Such usage suggests a common understanding of the term. While most Americans are not familiar with the different schools of thought within Islam, they are acquainted with fundamentalism in the Christian context, where the term is used in common parlance to refer, often negatively, to a certain brand of Christianity. When the term fundamentalism appears as an appendage of Islam, the reading public can only assume that the same connotations associated with Christian fundamentalism must also apply. Fundamentalism becomes a blanket term, shrouding Islam in Western perceptions of fundamentalism. In using the term, the media manages to associate large numbers of Muslim people with certain attitudes and behavior of a backward and inherently dangerous nature. In instances where the term fundamentalism is defined, stereotypical images are only reenforced, without specific mention of historical, political, social, or theological developments within Islam. Fundamentalism is applied as an essential term, implying that there is a certain characteristic, a core essence of the phenomenon, which transcends distinctions of specificity.

In understanding the current usage of fundamentalism, it would be a good idea to examine the connotations associated with the term and how the media is employing these connotations. We would have to ask if fundamentalism is indeed an essential phenomenon that can be applied universally to all religions, or if it has a more restricted meaning associated with a specific time and place? Does usage by the media reflect an exact meaning of the term or vague connotations surrounding the term? Is it appropriate to use fundamentalism in association with Islam or elements of Islam? Can a single term characterize Islam, or any religion, that includes within its fold many different inter-pretations of religious belief and practice? Finally, we would have to consider any distortions imposed by the current popular usage of fundamentalism by the media, possible political reasons for those distortions, and the possible ramifications of the continued employment of the term.

One of the few articles of late that actually attempts to define fundamentalism is Sullivan's "We Are at War." Sullivan defines fundamentalism as an element of many different religious faiths that is against freedom of thought and modernity. The author does not believe that all faiths are fundamentalist, but warns that there is an inherent tendency in monotheism, in the belief in one God, to foster oppression and terror against other faiths. Sul-livan states that fundamentalism composes a large element of the Islamic faith. The reason many people embrace fundamental-ism, he argues, is that it has a lot to offer:

> It elevates and comforts. It provides a sense of meaning and di-rection to those lost in a disorienting world. The blind re-course to texts embraced as literal truth, the injunction to fol-low the commandment of God before anything else, the sub-jugation of reason and judgment and even conscience to the dictates of dogma: these can be exhilarating and transforma-tive. They have led human beings to perform extraordinary acts of both good and evil. And they have an internal logic to them. If you believe that there is an eternal afterlife and that endless indescribable torture waits those who disobey God's law, then it requires no huge stretch of imagination to make sure that you not only conform to each dictate but that you also encourage and, if necessary, coerce others to do the same.[3]

According to Sullivan, in a world of absolutes, where truth in-volves the most important things imaginable—the meaning of life, the fate of one's soul, the difference between good and evil—there is no room for doubt, dissent, or choice. The article explains that fundamentalists are against freedom of thought and modernity; they want to forcibly impose their values on the rest of the world. They are at war with our way of life.

The term fundamentalism, as it happens, is also a very modern term. Men like Benjamin B. Warfield and Archibald Alexander Hodge formulated the basic theological position of Christian fundamentalism in the late 1880s at Princeton Theological Seminary. What they produced became known as Princeton theology, and it appealed to conservative Protestants who felt that modern trends such the social gospel movement, the historical and analytic study of the Bible, and attention to the theory of Darwin were a threat to their faith. In 1909 the brothers Milton and Lyman Stewart, whose wealth came from the oil industry, underwrote a project called the *Fundamentals*, a series of twelve paperback volumes published between 1910 and 1915. The *Fundamentals* drew up a bulwark of Christian beliefs to stand against onslaughts to the faith. Three million copies of the series were distributed.

The fundamental beliefs identified in the series can be reduced to five: (1) belief in the Bible as the literal word of God; (2) belief in the divinity of Christ and his virgin birth; (3) belief that Christ died on the Cross so that those who believe in him would be redeemed from sin; (4) belief in the literal resurrection of Christ from the dead; and (5) belief in Christ's return at the Second Coming. Fundamentalism as a unified and organized movement did not have a long life. People differing in their interpretations of certain aspects of fundamentalism departed from the movement and went their own way. Though the fundamentalist movement no longer exists, Christians who more or less agree on these fundamentals today are considered fundamentalists. You can find varying degrees of fundamentalist thought in many major denominations, representing different ideas and interpretations about the essentials of the Christian faith. There is no longer a single, unified Christian fundamentalist position.

Applying the term fundamentalist to people of other religions is problematic. In discussions of modern political developments in South Asia, scholars often make worried comments about Hindu fundamentalism. There has, however, never been a fundamentalist movement within Hinduism. Hinduism has not been reduced to a simple, concise confession of fundamental Hindu beliefs. In other words, there are no fundamentals of Hinduism in which to believe. The religion is extremely diverse. Yet certain Hindus, particularly politically active Hindu nationalists, including members of the dominant Bharatiya Janata Party (BJP), and right-wing groups such as the Rashtriya Swayamsevak Sangh (RSS) and the Vishva Hindu Parishad (VHP) are frequently referred to as Hindu fundamentalists. A leading scholar on such Hindu groups, Peter van der Veer, writes that though these groups claim to support a nationalism that embraces religion as the defining characteristic of the nation, they cannot be characterized as antimodernist movements.[4] Nationalism is part of the discourse of modernity and the project of Hindu nationalism is fundamentally modernist. Hindu nationalism, so-called Hindu fundamentalism, calls for interpretations of Hinduism based on Western understandings of religion in India and spring from Western conceptions of modernity.

If you apply the term fundamentalism to Islam, you would have to say that all Muslims are fundamentalists—that is, if you are defining fundamentalists as those who embrace certain essential beliefs of their faith. Every Muslim must accept five fundamental Islamic tenets, the five pillars of faith: belief in the one God and Muhammad as his prophet, the practice of giving alms to the poor, making the journey to Mecca at least once during one's lifetime, fasting during the month of Ramadan, and prayer. So, to the extent that all Muslims accept the five pillars of faith of Islam, all Muslims could be regarded as fundamentalists. The five pillars of Islamic faith say nothing, though, against freedom of thought. There is nothing in the basic tenets of the faith, nor in the Quran, that prohibits the embrace of modernity. Modernity, like many issues that fall outside the five pillars of faith, is subject to debate among Muslims. There is not a religious leader in Islam whose proclamations tell all Muslims what to believe. There are different interpretations of Islam and many differing voices of opinion on many issues. There is no single Islamic stance either for or against such matters as freedom of thought or modernity.

Islamic debate over elements of modernity is not a new phenomenon. An instance of difference of opinion among Muslims on the influence of Westernization, which mirrors similar debates today, took place in the late 1880s in India. The issue at hand was whether or not Muslim youth should receive a Western education. Under British colonialism of the time, neither Hindus nor Muslims were allowed political representation. In comparison with the British rulers of their land, most Indians lived in a state of degradation. Muslim reactions to the colonial situation in India varied. At the end of the nineteenth century, the Muslims of the subcontinent, while sharing a condition of subjugation, did not constitute a single united body. Islam was much more of a homogeneous religion than Hinduism in that all Muslims held a common belief in the five pillars of faith of Islam, but nevertheless differences existed among Muslims in India in regard to region, class, lineage, religious authority, and interpretation of Islam. There were Shia and Sunni Muslims and followers of various schools of thought within those two divisions of Islam; there were aristocratic Muslims, descendants of the rulers and administrators of the Mughal Empire, and there were extremely poor agriculturalists and Muslims of every shade in between.

With such differences among them, a single and common approach to the political, religious, and social conditions of the Muslim community of India as a whole was lacking. In the face of Western domination, Indian Muslims fragmented into different schools of thought that represented the various segments of the Muslim population, seeking to remedy the plight of Muslims in different ways. As the education required for employment in the British administration was one that reflected Western values and culture, the proper course of education for young Muslims became a leading question of the day among the upper classes.

Many Indian Muslims regarded Western education as having an insidious influence even when institutions did not actively promote acceptance of Christian ideas. Muslims had been slow to partake of education in British institutions of higher education. For Muslims, whose first duty was to learn the Quran, a liberal Western education, the study of English literature and history, was not only unnecessary, but was regarded by some as a threat to the purity of the faith.[5] Sir Syed Ahmad Khan, a leading promoter of Western education among Indian Muslims, believed that Muslims could never improve the condition of their lives under colonialism unless the *sharif*, the upper classes of Muslim society in India, were restored to an elevated position in government. In order to achieve this goal, a Western education proved a necessary tool of advancement under British colonial rule.

Sir Syed Ahmad Khan realized that for Muslims to be moved from their degraded status under colonialism, and for the Muslim community to be transformed into a vital force within the British empire, there had to be a theology that situated Muslims in the modern context. If Muslims saw their destiny as partners with the British in India, if they had faith that it was Allah's will that they achieve a dominant place in the secular administration of India, they could be moved to accept Western education as a tool for their success. But faith was the force through which deeds were done, and a theology that gave the Muslims authority to function in the modern context was missing. Sir Syed provided this theology in his teaching that Western education did not contradict faith in Islam. On the contrary, it was the duty of Muslims under the law of God to take their place at the helm of worldly learning. Sir Syed undertook the writing of a new commentary on the Quran that supported this position. He showed how the acquisition of Western knowledge was the only viable means for Muslims to rise from their inferior status under colonialism.

Though the commentary was widely rejected by Muslims, Sir Syed Ahmad Khan continued his efforts to modernize Islam by introducing Western education to his community. In June 1875, he opened the first Muslim institution of higher education dedicated to Western education in India. The Muhammadan Anglo-Oriental College was founded in Aligarh, about eighty miles from Delhi. From the founding of the college there were hopes for the establishment of a university, hopes that were realized in 1920 when the Government of India granted a charter to Aligarh Muslim University. Initially, many Muslims in India were strongly opposed to Sir Syed Ahmad Khan's plans for the college and few Muslims were interested in sending their sons to Aligarh. Many Muslims condemned Sir Syed to the extent that *fatwas* of *kufr* (declarations of infidelity to the faith) were issued against him from Mecca. Orthodox members of the community ostracized Sir Syed for his promulgation of Western education and for his association with the British.

Slowly the validity of the college came to be accepted by more Muslims. The British Education Commission of 1882 reported growing approval among Indian Muslims for Sir Syed Ahmad Khan's educational efforts. The report of the commission explained that as much as Indian Muslims venerated the traditions of their forefathers and prized the treasures of a copious and elegant literature of Islam, they had gradually come to see that the only education able to lift their culture to a status of equality with the British empire and restore it to a position of influence was an "education frankly acknowledging the advance of science, catholic in its sympathies with all that was admirable in the literature, history and philosophy of other countries, broad in its outlines and exact in its studies."[6] As acceptance of Syed Ahmad's ideas grew, *fatwas* were issued, but they were now in his support. Maulana Shah Sulaiman Chishti of Ajmer, a major Islamic figure in India, issued a *fatwa* declaring that any contributions made to Syed Ahmad's Muslim college would be considered meritorious. They would be considered gifts to the faith. After 1886 it began to be apparent that public opinion among Muslims had turned in favor of Syed Ahmad, the Aligarh College, and Western education.

The debate over the appropriateness of Western education among Indian Muslims could be considered a debate over modernism, as Western education represented the forces of modernism in India in the 1800s. There were differing opinions. There was not a fundamental Islamic stance on education. There was at first strong opposition to Western education. Considering that this debate took place during a time of Western political and ideological domination of India, under conditions of harsh colonial rule, it is no great wonder that Muslims might have rejected the education demanded by the British rulers. But the rejection of Western education was subject to debate among Muslims. The issue was not strictly religious. Nor was it simply a matter of rejection or acceptance of modernity. It was political and economic. On one side there was a position that held that Western education only served to strengthen the hold of Western imperialism. On the other hand it was argued that Western education would give Muslims access to economic and political power within the British empire. The very fact that there was a debate should correct any misunderstanding that antimodernism is a fundamental Islamic position.

Muslims today are debating similar issues regarding the influence of Westernization on Islamic cultures. Often the issues are enmeshed in political and economic concerns. Other than the few basic religious suppositions shared by all Muslims, there is no fundamental Islamic stance for all matters, in all times, and all places. Contrary to various representations in the media, there is no such thing as a single worldwide Islamic nation, as there is not a nation composed only of people who believe in Jesus Christ or Lord Ram. There are differences of opinion between Muslims on issues of political and religious leadership, as well as a host of other matters. During the partition of India in 1947, for instance, two sections of India were lopped off and declared to be Pakistan, a Muslim-majority nation. It was not long, however, before a civil war ensued, resulting in the birth of the new nation of Bangladesh. Within both countries, Pakistan and Bangladesh, political rivalries between powerful interest groups are as fierce as they are in the United States. There is no such thing as overall political unity among Muslims in a single country, much less across the entire globe.

What is happening when articles in a highly respected and widely distributed U.S. publication like the *New York Times* reflect a perception of a single, homogeneous Islamic nation operating in the world, one that is described as largely composed of fundamentalists? An interview with Nobel laureate V. S. Naipaul, which appeared in an edition of the *New York Times Magazine*, further fuels this misunderstanding of Islam.[7] In the interview, Naipaul describes Islam as having an imperial drive to extend its reach and to root out the unbeliever, to destroy anything that does not conform to Islamic thinking. The interviewer understands Naipaul to be speaking only about fundamentalist Islam and therefore asks Naipaul what he thinks about nonfundamentalist

Islam. Naipaul responds that there is no such thing as nonfundamentalist Islam. It would be a contradiction. In clarifying himself, he states that the most important thing in Islam is paradise, heaven, and that no one can be moderate about wanting to go to heaven. Naipaul then adds that for this reason there are no moderate Muslim governments. They are all fundamentalists. The picture that emerges for the American public is that the face of the enemy is Islamic.

Fundamentalism is a Christian theological movement related to specific events, places, and people. Christian fundamentalism should not be applied indiscriminately to Christian charismatic movements, Christian conservatism, or evangelicalism, though it has connections with these. But fundamentalism has come to be employed very loosely. The term "fundamentalist" is seldom defined specifically, but it is almost always used derogatively. Implied in the term fundamentalism is all that is oppressive, bigoted, and antimodern in religion, regardless of the faith. Members of other religions such as Hindus and Muslims, erroneously described as fundamentalists in popular journalism, are thus depicted in a negative light. Vague assumptions regarding fundamentalism widely accepted in the West as descriptive of Islam, include the idea that fundamentalists are against freedom of thought and modernity.

The rhetoric that attributes a dangerous and oppressive characteristic to a large and specific group of people is the rhetoric of war. It is an inhumane rhetoric, portraying millions of innocent people as the enemy. Muslims have long been subject to this kind of portrayal. Most U.S. citizens have never lived in a Muslim country. They have never been intimate friends with Muslim storekeepers, farmers, grandparents, and children. They have most likely never seen a Muslim portrayed as a good and noble figure in movies, on television, or in Western literature. If a Muslim appears on the TV screen, he or she will appear as a menacing character, wearing a gun belt and bearing a raised fist. The American public has long been subject to such negative portrayals, which severely distort and manipulate the lives of one in every five humans on earth (the approximate population of Muslims).

The use of the derogatory term "fundamentalist" to pinpoint the enemy in the current crisis is not too dissimilar from the rhetoric used in attacks throughout history. During the Cold War, all citizens of the USSR were dangerous "commies." As most Americans did not know any citizens of the USSR and knew nothing about the politics of the country, we were not immune to such all-encompassing propaganda. All the Jews of Europe, every man, woman, and child, were characterized as rubbish, absolute rubbish by the Nazi regime. To the Spanish conquistadors, native American Indians were less than human; they had no soul. In all cases of such dehumanization of the enemy, the point is to legitimate nothing less than the extinction of another people.

Are fundamentalists our enemy in the current crisis? Fundamentalism loosely defined can refer to a great horde. There are millions of people in the world with deeply entrenched religious worldviews. If we include as our enemy everyone who fits into the vague stereotypical image of a fundamentalist, the enemy looms very large. As globalization brings competing worldviews closer and closer, there is a tendency, it seems, for people to want to affirm their distinctiveness. Where we might think others would welcome the flood of images, ideas, and products from the West, to many the onslaught of Westernization threatens to bring about a disintegration of their own culture and identity. Thus we see the rise of movements around the world that attempt to strengthen a collective sense of uniqueness.[8] Religion, which is closely interwoven with other aspects of society, is often held up as a badge of honor, as the defining characteristic of the culture. Should we regard all these people, including those Americans who place religion at the center of their worldview and their politics, as enemies?

In defining fundamentalists as enemies, are we saying that such people have no place in the modern world? Are we denying them the right to self-identity and the right to embrace a worldview of their own selection? Must they embrace Western conceptions of modernity or else become branded as fundamental enemies? Can freedom of thought be applied only to expressions that correspond to the liberal Western ideology? Has liberal thought become so imperialistic? Questioning the boundaries of Western hegemony does not imply total relativity; it does not imply that the ideologies of totalitarian governments, for instance, have an equal right of expression. It certainly does not condone murder. But it should lead us to consider the implications of and the ideology behind the targeting of worldviews that do not correspond to our own, especially those that are branded fundamentalist. It should lead us to abandon the use of the term fundamentalist as a category into which we shove large numbers of Muslims.

Are we in a war? That depends on your perspective. Life is a constant negotiation of boundaries. In a pluralist world, there are bound to be struggles. To be at war you have to identify a common enemy, someone wholly Other, whose very existence threatens your own. The media and political rhetoric clearly mark the enemy, dividing the world into two camps, theirs and ours. This is the language of terror, the rhetoric of war. The language of the media, speaking to a vast American audience, seems to mirror the stereotypical mind-set of the fundamentalist. It labels those whose opinions, beliefs, culture, and politics are dissimilar to our own as the enemy, stirring emotional fervor and calls for war. If we whip up a rhetoric of war in which not only our lives, but also our souls are at stake, we should not be at all surprised to see bombs falling in our name.

**NOTES**

1. Andrew Sullivan, "We Are at War," *New York Times*, October 7, 2001.
2. Daniel Golden, "Rewriting History: Attack Causes Panic for Textbook Authors," *Wall Street Journal*, October 9, 2001.
3. Sullivan, "We Are at War."
4. Peter van der Veer, *Religious Nationalism: Hindus and Muslims in India* (Berkeley: University of California Press, 1994), 132–33.
5. David Lelyveld, *Aligarh's First Generation: Muslim Solidarity in British India* (Princeton: Princeton University Press, 1978), 87.
6. Cited in *Morison's History of the M.A.O. College, Aligarh*, ed. Safi Ahmad Kakorwi (Lucknow: Markaz-e-Adab-e-Urdu, 1988), 17ff.
7. Adam Shartz, "Literary Criticism: Questions for V. S. Naipaul," *New York Times Magazine*, October 28, 2001: 19.
8. Thomas Hylland Erikson, "Globalization and the Politics of Identity," *United Nations Chronicle*, Autumn 1999 (http://folk.uio.no/geirthe /UNChron.html).

**SUGGESTIONS FOR FURTHER READING**

Ford, Peter. "Why Do They Hate Us?" *Christian Science Monitor*, September 27, 2001 (http://www.csmonitor.com/2001/0927/p1s1-wogi.html).
Jurgensmeyer, Mark. *Terror in the Mind of God: The Global Rise of Religious Violence.* Berkeley: University of California Press, 2000.
Keen, Sam. *Faces of the Enemy: Reflections of the Hostile Imagination.* San Francisco: Harper and Row, 1986.
Schiffauer, Werner. "Production of Fundamentalism: On the Dynamics of Producing the Radically Different." In *Religion and Media*, ed. Hent De Vries and Samuel Weber (Stanford: Stanford University Press, 2001).

Zone 4, *Hero*. *Reprinted with the permission of Zone 4.*

# 8. Jihad

Kenneth Church

One of the still unanswered but crucial questions about 9/11 is how the world's impoverished citizens regard that attack on global capitalism and the U.S. military-industrial complex as well as the subsequent U.S.–led invasion of Afghanistan. In order to prevent too much reflection on the symbolic potency of the unfolding conflict, the U.S. government has cast the conflict in terms of "the war on terrorism," "civilization" versus "barbarism," "good" against "evil," or "just war" against "holy war" or *jihad.* Jihad evokes images of Muslim fanatics wielding weapons (preferably of foreign make) in acts of terrorism designed to impose an oppressive Islamic regime wherever they can. By labeling bin Laden's jihad against the United States as simply terrorism, the Bush Administration effectively strips its perpetrators of actual political grievances or aspirations and seeks to isolate them from the main community of Muslim believers. In turn, deployment of this rhetorical strategy allows the United States and the more loyal (Western) members of the fragile coalition to conduct their own version of a holy war to defend and spread their virulent vision of civilization whose meaning and membership they largely control. Civilization (in the singular) opposes bin Laden's uncompromising Islamic order, and much of the world's population struggles to find their place in neither. The following exposition of jihad, therefore, aims to situate the current use of the term in a broader historical context in order to illuminate its multiple meanings and to demonstrate how the fixation on the notion of jihad as armed struggle conceals the larger social, economic, and political issues underlying the present conflict. In essence, the narrow definition of jihad that prevails in the press has little to do with either the specific political concerns of those who declare jihad or the larger global struggle over inequitable distributions of power and wealth.

## Foundational Meanings of Jihad in History

In the sacred sources of Islam—the Quran and *hadiths*—jihad generally means a "striving in the path of God." The Quran is the most sacred text of Islam because it is the word of God or Allah as revealed in Arabic to His messenger, Muhammad, by the angel Gabriel over a span of twenty-two years from 610 until Muhammad's death in 632 C.E. As the word of the one and only God, the contents of the Quran are transcendant or true for all time and space. And yet, as a set of revelations conveyed to the mortal, fully human, messenger Muhammad, the contents address specific events rendering the word of Allah historical. Hence, the general obligation to wage jihad is at once transcendant and historical, and this dual nature has endowed the term with several meanings as derived from specific revelations recorded in the Quran. The *hadiths* and jurists among the *ulama*, or learned men of Islam, subsequently divided those injunctions to carry on jihad into an internal and external struggle.[1]

The Quran makes the internal striving in the path of Allah incumbent upon each Muslim. "And strive for Allah with the endeavour which is His right. He hath chosen you and hath not laid upon you in religion any hardship; the faith of your father Abraham (is yours). He hath named you Muslims of old time and in this (Scripture). . . . So establish worship, pay the poor-due, and hold fast to Allah." Or again: "And whosoever striveth, striveth only for himself, for lo! Allah is altogether Independent of (His) creatures."[2] These verses emphasize that the surest testament of the faith of Muslims, or those who have submitted to the will of Allah, is their acceptance of the individual struggle to realize that will throughout their lives by upholding all that is good and abjuring evil.[3] At the time of these revelations in seventh-century Arabia, the Islamic injunction to assume responsibility for upholding Allah's will through inner jihad, rather than seeking recourse in one's lineage or tribal affiliation was intended to affirm the goodness of a human being. Similarly, this command was a powerful witness to the eternal, transcendant existence of the one God, Allah. While a believer could most clearly manifest his or her submission through observation of the five pillars of Islam, the Quran and *hadiths* illuminated how in fact submission was a complete way of life that should pervade an individual's day-to-day affairs.[4] The magnitude of this inner struggle explains its designation as the "greater jihad."

Given the all-encompassing submission expected of a believer, the invocation to carry on an inner struggle easily translated into calls to conduct an external jihad as a witness for the faith. "Ye should believe in Allah and His messenger, and should strive for the cause of Allah with your wealth and your lives." Or more boldly: "Go forth, light-armed and heavy-armed, and strive with your wealth and your lives in the way of Allah!"[5] The first verse could be construed to mean that one should bear witness to the faith by committing one's possessions and life to the cause in any number of ways, thereby underscoring the social, political, and religious commitment of each Muslim to realize the will of God during one's life on earth. The second verse explicitly calls upon the sacrifice of wealth and life in armed struggle to defend and spread the faith. This latter depiction of external jihad as armed struggle underscores how each Muslim was part of a community of believers, the *umma*, that must defend itself collectively against outside aggression and seek converts among the "heathens" (meaning primarily pastoral polytheists).

Because the community of believers, from its foundation, was both religious and political in nature, any kind of striving waged on behalf of the community and faith was at once religious and political. The history of the *umma* under Muhammad's leadership, particularly after the emigration (*hijra*) to Medina in 622, abounds with armed struggle against polytheist Arab tribes and the Jews in Medina and neighboring settlements.[6] These struggles expressed both the need to defend the precarious existence of the *umma* as a religious and political community and the desire to spread the word of Allah among nonbelievers. Where warfare was concerned, the Quran, *hadiths*, and subsequent juridical pronouncements by members of the *ulama* elaborated a set of prescriptions and prohibitions governing how Muslims could conduct holy war.[7] This notion of external jihad, centered around the idea of spreading the faith primarily through peaceful means, became known as the "lesser jihad."

The period of rapid conquest (632–751) following Muhammad's death, which brought lands from Central Asia to Spain under Islamic rule, was viewed by Muslims as testimony to the triumph of Allah's will in human history. This rapid spread of a universalistic faith was an unprecedented event in human history and underscored to Muslims the power of Allah's existence. The success of the conquest rested in part on the execution of jihad that the Arab conquerors conducted not just with the sword, but also through the authority of the word as compiled in the Quran and taught by members of the *ulama*, as well as with the power of personal example manifested in commercial transactions, governance, and the observation of the five pillars. To be sure, this was a period of taking Islam to the nonbelievers, of expanding the "abode of Islam" (*dar al-Islam*) against the "abode of war" (*dar al-harb*) that lay beyond the lands governed by Muslim rulers. It would be wrong, however, to view the call to expand the domains of Islam and the attendant process of conversion as simply a military manifestation of jihad.

The success of the conquest brought to the fore a third meaning or application of jihad. In addition to the notion of internal striving and external struggle with nonbelievers to enjoin them to convert, jihad also came to embrace efforts to return to the purity of the faith in the face of perceived deviations by one or another group *within* the community of believers. That is, members of the *ulama* who felt threatened by or otherwise abhorred the apparent deviant practices and beliefs of fellow converts occasionally undertook a revivalist jihad in an attempt to bring those deviant Muslims back to the true path of Islam as delineated by Islamic law or *sharia*. This exhortation to reform has deep roots in Islamic history dating back to the Quran itself. Indeed, in a general sense, the Quran construes Islam as a final, definitive reform of the Judaeo-Christian prophetic tradition. God's revelations to Muhammad represent the final effort to return the followers of the Judaeo-Christian prophetic tradition, and by extension humanity at large, to the true path of divine illumination through revelation of the Word of God to the final messenger, Muhammad. Within the *umma*, initiatives to revive the moral integrity of the revelation occurred as early as the seventh century with the Shiite separation from the Sunnis, for instance.[8]

This discussion of jihad underscores that the sacred texts of Islam and, subsequently, members of the *ulama* or community of scholars reinforced the notion that jihad constituted an inherent obligation of Muslims to strive to uphold the faith internally and externally. No single, precise definition of the term, however, was ever promulgated by a central religious text or authority, including the Quran itself. Rather, multiple renditions of this injunction were elaborated, depending on the specific circumstances surrounding Muhammad's recitation of the relevant revelation or a jurist's subsequent interpretation of that revelation. Scholars came to understand the various meanings of striving as a jihad of the heart, tongue, hand, and sword.

Indeed, even if jihad was seen as a sacred duty, it was never considered an official (sixth) pillar of Islam by a majority of Muslims precisely because of its multiple meanings. This exposition also highlights a profound difference between the organization of religious authority under Islam and Christianity. In the Christian world—particularly in its Catholic and Orthodox guise—a centralized ecclesiastical structure exists for each variant of the faith that has allowed the proclamation of incontrovertible doctrinal positions. No such centralized structure has governed the organization of the *ulama* in the Islamic world, thereby rendering even more difficult the delineation of a uniform definition of jihad.

## Jihad in the Modern Period of European Imperial Domination

In light of jihad's diverse meanings as a striving in the path of God, it is not surprising to find that as the community of the faithful grew, fragmented politically, and encountered outside powers that challenged the integrity of the Islamic world, scholars emphasized one aspect or another of jihad in response to changing circumstances. One could correlate pronouncements about jihad by Muslim scholars and rulers in different Islamic lands across time with changes in their communities in terms of their perceptions of the moral condition of the Muslim populations, religious divisions in the *umma*, incursions by foreign powers like the European crusaders beginning in the eleventh century, or opportunities to expand the boundaries of the "abode of Islam." By the nineteenth century, however, European imperial powers became embroiled in a fierce competition over territorial expansion which, by the end of the century, yielded them control over most of the lands of Islam from Africa to Indonesia, while parts of the Ottoman empire, Arabia, Iran, and Afghanistan remained independent.

This profound change in the political, economic, and social configuration of the world of Islam sparked numerous militant jihads against the European imposition of infidel rule. These uprisings ranged from West Africa (Senegal-Mali) across North Africa (Algeria, Sudan), to the Caucasus (Chechnia and Daghestan), India, and Sumatra and Java in Indonesia. All were relatively short-lived, regional in scope, and defensive in objective, seeking to retain a fragile autonomy against European aggression. Several of the jihads sought to establish Islamic states amidst local, non-Muslim populations. Hence, despite their Islamic foundations, these militant jihads were not at all unified but rather reflected the differences in objectives, diversity of cultures, limitation of resources and communications, and the differences between imperial powers. At the same time, it should be pointed out that the impetus for several of these defensive jihads came from their leaders' performing the *hajj*, or pilgrimage to Mecca, in fulfillment of one of the five pillars of Islam. This annual event allowed Muslims from all over the world to meet and discuss the political and social conditions of their respective lands and to return with new sources of inspiration for defending and reviving the faith in accordance with *sharia*.

Indeed, while manifestations of militant jihad against the infidel captured the attention of Muslims and Europeans alike, as occurred with the twenty-five-year war of liberation waged by the Imam Shamyl in Chechnia and Daghestan against the Russians

(1834–59), a more profound response to Western domination took the form of revivalist and modernist movements. Revivalists like Muhammad ibn Abd al-Wahhab (1703–92) of Arabia sought to restore the spiritual vigor of Islam by returning to the purity of the sacred texts in order to redress the decline in morals and the corruption of religious practices that he perceived around him. He undertook a jihad of tongue and sword against all those who did not abide by his vision of pure Islam, including fellow Sunni and Shiite Muslims, and destroyed the sacred tombs of the Prophet Muhammad, Husayn, and several prominent Sufis for allegedly fostering idolatry among Muslims.[9] His was a strident revivalist jihad that has provided the religious foundation of the Saudi regime and inspiration to Osama bin Laden as well.

Modernist movements differed from this type of revivalism by seeking to reinvigorate their faith by cultivating the old tradition of philosophical inquiry, scientific reflection, and social dynamism that characterized the early centuries of Islam. Reformers like Jamal al-Din al-Afghani (1838–97) from Iran and Muhammad Iqbal (1875–1938), who is regarded as the spiritual father of Pakistan, embarked on jihads of the heart and pen to defend Muslims against Western hegemony. They advocated revitalizing scientific inquiry and borrowing appropriate technologies and institutional forms like the nation-state for this purpose. For them and many others, Islam was not somehow incompatible with "the modern world" but indeed could boast a rich history of scientific scholarship, technological innovation, and commercial prosperity that needed to be emancipated from a conservative *ulama* and defended against the secular, self-serving powers of Europe.

As suggested by this cursory survey of Muslims' responses to European imperial domination, jihad in the modern era assumed the same forms as prescribed in the Quran but was infused with new content and aims that reflected the profound transformation of the world from the days of the Prophet

Muhammad. Imperial rule and capitalist economic development and exploitation provoked or inspired numerous calls for jihad, each of which must be understood within the specific era and place where it occurred. That is, each stemmed from distinct political, social, and economic conditions. Wars of liberation against infidel rulers, revivalist campaigns against fellow Muslims and nonbelievers, rigorous formulations of self-criticism, extensive social reform programs to promote education, employment, and emancipation—all have expressed jihad in the age of European domination and illuminate both the vitality of Islam as a universal faith in this age of globalization as well as the multiple Islams that invigorate diverse lands.

This was precisely the point stressed by Edward Said when he wrote shortly after the events of September 11, "there isn't a single Islam: there are Islams, just as there are Americas. This diversity is true of all traditions, religions or nations even though some of their adherents have futilely tried to draw boundaries around themselves and pin their creeds down neatly."[10] Instances of military jihad in this period represent efforts to defend the faith against perceived foreign aggression rather than campaigns to expand through violence the "abode of Islam" (*dar al-Islam*) into the domains of the infidel. As is readily apparent, the growth of the *umma* to a billion people who reside throughout the world is not the result of military expansion but of a complex array of processes associated with decolonization, the collapse of the Soviet Union, and the forging of a global capitalist economy that has entailed immense social and economic dislocation inasmuch as it has made the world smaller and more integrated.

## Jihad after September 11

A crucial question that arises in the wake of September 11, therefore, is how Muslims understand the sacred, transcendant obligation to undertake jihad in this new era of international crisis. In one sense, the conflict between Osama bin Laden and the United States centers on jihad. How can each side utilize jihad for its purposes? On the other hand, from the perspective of the United Nations and the call for a dialogue "between civilizations," the power of 9/11 transcends the boundaries of Islam and reduces the role of jihad.

Within the world of Islam, since the events of 9/11, Osama bin Laden has expanded his political diatribes against the United States to include not just the demand that the United States abandon its bases in Saudi Arabia and terminate its support of tyrannical princedoms in the Gulf states; he has increasingly embraced the Palestinian cause against Israel as the linchpin of his politics so as to win wider support among (mostly Arab) Muslims, primarily in the Middle East. The recent decision by the Bush Administration to place Hizbollah, Hamas, and Islamic Jihad on its list of terrorist organizations only strengthens his case, as many newspapers in the Middle East immediately denounced the decision and called into question the administration's definition of terrorism.

From the vantage point of many Muslims in the region, the jihad espoused by these organizations represents national liberation movements. Thus, the U.S. government's decision runs the risk of fulfilling an apparent strategic goal of bin Laden: namely, to forge stronger ties between these local militant jihads in Palestine, Lebanon, Egypt, Pakistan, and beyond the Middle East, as in Indonesia, in a bid to foment a larger unified jihad focused against the United States. Surely the hydra-headed al-Qaeda network, which allegedly operates in sixty countries, provides logistical support and personnel for such an endeavor. From their vantage point, these militant struggles in their local incarnations and more generally directed against the United States are defensive, as bin Laden understands the attacks in New York and Washington, D.C. The U.S. presence in the Persian Gulf, its support of sanctions against Iraq, its heretofore unilateral support of Israel, and its war against the Taliban all represent offensive positions or campaigns against the Muslim world.

At the same time, bin Laden seems keenly aware that the vast majority of Muslims do not support his acts of violence directed against the infidel United States. Rather, insofar as he has assiduously cultivated the image of a holy warrior, clad in military fatigues, wielding a kalashnikov, and speaking his mind by rock facades in the manner of a humble but defiant religious leader, he represents himself as one dedicated to the violent removal of the United States from Muslim lands, the ultimate martyr for the faith. Casting himself in this role, how can he not insist to the world that he has nuclear weapons as a deterrent to the nuclear threat posed by the United States?[11] But he also seems to understand that this image can resonate deeply with many Muslims who may loathe his violence and deplore the type of Islamic state he may aspire to establish.[12] Not more than a few thousand Pakistanis crossed into Afghanistan to join the Taliban's jihad against the United States.

Nonetheless, the collapse of the Soviet Union has brought into bolder relief the nature of the U.S. presence in the Middle East as one primarily devoted to facilitating and defending the extraction of fossil fuels and getting them to market, even if this enterprise requires the defense of regimes like the house of Saud whose human rights record has been vehemently criticized by organizations like Amnesty International. It is precisely these features of the U.S. presence in the region that raise bin Laden's hopes that many Muslims will support a jihad of the heart, pen, and hand against the United States in defense of the Holy Land, the rights of the Palestinians, and broader issues of social justice stemming from the glaring poverty throughout the land.

For its part, the Bush Administration has construed bin Laden's jihad as an attack on "civilization as we know it" under the banner of "the war on terrorism." But from the outset, this stance has placed the administration in an awkward position. This type of rhetoric removes the conflict from the world of Islam. Efforts to obtain retributive justice through the bombing campaign in Afghanistan replete with "bunker busters" and "daisy cutters" are seen as a war against evil that terrorists seek to spread in the world to people of all faiths, including Muslims. According to this view, bin Laden and company are not Muslims, a stance President Bush took in his opening address to the United Nations when he declared: "They dare to ask God's blessing as they set out to kill innocent men, women and children. But the God of Isaac and Ishmael would never answer such a prayer. And a murderer is not a martyr. He is just a murderer."[13] Muslims do not stand for such terrorist acts nor oppressive regimes like that of the Taliban, he suggests.

Interestingly, in an effort to demonstrate how the Taliban and bin Laden are not the only Muslims capable of mounting a militant jihad, the Northern Alliance declared its own jihad in overrunning Mazar-e-Sharif. This tactic, which the Bush Administration most certainly supported, serves to isolate the Taliban, bin Laden, and his supporters in al-Qaeda. Similarly, Secretary of State Colin Powell's request that Muslim countries like Turkey and Indonesia supply peace-keeping forces to help stabilize Afghanistan in the post-Taliban era further isolates these foes. The decree establishing military tribunals to try any foreign terrorists also deprives them of the opportunity of using their trials as a forum to publicize their political views.

Finally, it seems apparent that in addition to the "lesser jihad" that the administration has cautiously supported against the Taliban, the U.S. government is intent on fostering a "greater jihad" of the heart and pen. This jihad entails inner reflection and self-

criticism among Muslims as part of a larger collective contempla-
tion of why they have abided such terrorists in their midst and not
fostered more democratic governments in their lands.[14] It also
confines such self-reflection to the more manageable unit of individual nation-states. Taken together, these tactics and rhetorical
positions deny bin Laden and other militant Islamic organizations
their own histories and political agendas. And to ensure that the
Muslim world understands this, the administration has under-
taken the largest propaganda campaign since World War II, one
that includes tapping the talent of Hollywood to fashion a strategy
to counter bin Laden's growing appeal in the Muslim world.[15]

On the other hand, the Bush Administration and others do
not wish to dissociate Islam from their war on terrorism. To be
sure, the president quickly learned to refrain from calling the
war a "crusade," in order to galvinize support from Muslim nations for his international coalition against terrorism. And yet his
repeated call for God's blessing at the end of his speeches and
references to the strength of "our faith" imparts a particularly
Christian cast to his idea of civilization. Furthermore, the association of militant jihad with terrorism (except for U.S.–backed jihads like that of the Northern Alliance) reinforces the role of
Islam in the present conflict. This stigmatization raises the scim-
itar of "holy war" against "just war." The rhetoric of terrorism
identifies expressions of militant jihad with barbarism, and by de-
priving its proponents of legitimate political grievances, this
stance renders more difficult the arduous task of reconsidering
U.S. policies in the Middle East in an effort to win the long-term
support of the Muslim population there and elsewhere.

In effect, the United States has embarked on a secular, highly
militarized holy war of its own that increasingly bears some of the
characteristics of the jihad we have deemed evil and terrorist. In
the name of national security and civilization, the Bush Administration exhorts U.S. citizens to conduct themselves with the

utmost vigilance in seeking out enemies within their midst.[16] The hastily passed PATRIOT Act bolsters the foundation for an assault on civil liberties, certainly not akin to what bin Laden advocates, but oppressive all the same and dependent on a culture of fear. And the use of such weapons as the "daisy cutter" mirrors the use of planes as missiles in their destructive capabilities if not degree of carnage. Both sides proclaim the righteousness of their cause, insist on the defensiveness of their purpose, and deploy weapons of mass destruction, the effect of which is intended to make us fixate on holy war as the nature of the conflict. But for the Bush Administration, focused as it is on elections, the health of the economy, and the return to unfettered consumerism (otherwise known as "normalcy"), time is of the essence in the prosecution of its holy war.

The longer the conflict persists as armed struggle, the greater the risk that an increasing number of global citizens will recognize that it cannot be resolved by holy war, indeed has little to do with jihad at base, and requires international consensus garnered through international organizations, and not the U.S.–led coalition. As so many commentators throughout the world have already made clear, the foundations of the current holy war rest on poverty and social injustice, not evil and terrorism.

### NOTES

1. The term *hadith* refers to a written record about the words and actions, or the tradition (*sunna*) of the messenger Muhammad. Religious scholars, the *ulama,* collected and verified the contents and chain of transmission of these traditions after the death of Muhammad, primarily in the eighth and ninth centuries, C.E.

2. *The Meaning of the Glorious Koran,* Mohammed Marmaduke Pickthall, trans. (New York: Mentor, no date): sura XXII, verse 78, p. 247, and XXIX:6, p. 285.

3. Islam literally means "submission to the will of Allah."

4. The five pillars of Islam include the profession of the creed, "There

is no god but Allah, and Muhammad is the Messenger of Allah"; prayer five times a day; the giving of alms as acknowledgment of one's social responsibility for the welfare of the community; performing the fast during the holy month of Ramadan; and undertaking the *hajj* or pilgrimage to Mecca if one is physically and financially able.

5. LXI:11, p. 398; IX:41, p. 149.

6. Thus, a verse of a sura revealed to Muhammad at Medina declares: "Warfare is ordained for you, though it is hateful unto you; but it may happen that ye hate a thing which is good for you, and it may happen that ye love a thing which is bad for you. Allah knoweth, ye know not." II:216, p. 52.

7. These included, for example, prescriptions for the type of person able to wage military jihad (healthy, loyal, devout males), the command not to kill women and children, the issuance of an invitation to join the *umma* before commencing combat, and so on. For a description of these prescriptions and prohibitions, see Majid Khadduri, *War and Peace in the Law of Islam* (Baltimore: Johns Hopkins University Press, 1955).

8. A tradition of the Prophet Muhammad states that Allah will send renewers of the faith to the *umma* at the beginning of every century. For an exposition of the roots of revivalism, see John L. Esposito, *Islam: The Straight Path* (New York: Oxford University Press, 1988), 115–18.

9. Husayn was the son of Ali ibn Abi Talib, the cousin and son-in-law of the Prophet Muhammad. Ali was the fourth caliph or "successor" to Muhammad, but many of his partisans regarded him as the only legitimate successor. They argued that succession should have been based on Ali's blood relation to the Prophet rather than on the selection of the appropriate candidate by the *umma*, which meant by the leaders of the community, namely, the *ulama*. This latter group would become known as "Sunni" Muslims, whose leader, the Caliph Yazid, murdered Husayn in 680, thereby consolidating the division between Sunnis and Shiites or "partisans of Ali." Abd al-Wahhab's destruction of Husayn's tomb in the eighteenth century served only to exacerbate tensions between Sunnis and Shiites.

10. Edward Said, "Islam and the West Are Inadequate Banners," *Observer*, 16 September 2001.

11. Tim Weaver, "Bin Laden Has Nuclear Arms, He Tells Paper," *New York Times* (10 November 2001).

12. See, for instance, Peter Ford, "Why Do They Hate Us?" *Christian Science Monitor* (27 September 2001); and Orhan Pamuk, "The Anger of the Damned," *New York Review of Books* (15 November 2001): 12.

13. "In Bush's Words: Nations Must Resist 'Decisively and Collectively,'" *New York Times* (11 November 2001).

14. For an expression of such critical self-reflection, see Jeff Jacoby,

"Islamic Moderates Denounce Fanatics," *Boston Globe* (12 November 2001). See also Thomas L. Friedman, "World War III," *New York Times* (13 September 2001).

15. Elizabeth Becker, "In the War on Terrorism, a Battle to Shape Public Opinion," *New York Times* (11 November 2001).

16. The anthrax attacks have accentuated the calls for greater domestic vigilance, including using the internet for a more comprehensive surveillance system. James R. Pinkerton, "Use Internet as a Defense System," *Newsday*, reprinted in *Watertown Times* (12 November 2001): 5.

### SUGGESTIONS FOR FURTHER READING

Esposito, John L. *Islam: The Straight Path.* New York: Oxford University Press, 1988.

Hodgson, Marshall G. S. *The Venture of Islam: Conscience and History in a World Civilization,* 3 vols. Chicago: University of Chicago Press, 1974.

Kelsay, John, and James Turner Johnson, eds. *Just War and Jihad: Historical and Theoretical Perspectives on War and Peace in Western and Islamic Traditions.* New York: Greenwood Press, 1991.

Lapidus, Ira M. *A History of Islamic Societies.* Cambridge: Cambridge University Press, 1988.

Partner, Peter. *God of Battles: Holy Wars of Christianity and Islam.* Princeton: Princeton University Press, 1997.

Peters, F. E. *A Reader on Classical Islam.* Princeton: Princeton University Press, 1994.

Peters, Rudolph. *Jihad in Classical and Modern Islam.* Princeton: Markus Weiner Publishers, 1996.

Tibi, Bassam. *The Challenge of Fundamentalism: Political Islam and the New World Order.* Berkeley: University of California Press, 1998.

Voll, John Obert. *Islam: Continuity and Change in the Modern World.* Syracuse: Syracuse University Press, 1994.

# 9. Justice

ERIN MCCARTHY

Since September 11, the term "justice" has often appeared alongside "peace." In his address to the nation the evening of 9/11, President Bush stated, "This is a day when all Americans from every walk of life unite in our resolve for justice and peace." Yet the term "justice" was not and has not been defined, and, as many critically minded citizens around the world have noted, the brand of "justice" the president, the CIA, the military, and the media seem to be advocating does not necessarily go hand in hand with peace. In what follows, I discuss two types of justice that have been at work in the current dialogue surrounding the events of 9/11: retributive justice and frontier justice. These two types of justice are also being used alongside the idea of a "just" war. Finally, I introduce the concept of restorative justice, which is not at play in the current dialogue, but which, I argue, holds the most powerful tools for uniting the resolve for peace.

Perhaps the classic (Western) definition of justice comes largely from the *Republic*, one of ancient Greek philosopher Plato's most influential works. Plato recounts a conversation between his teacher Socrates and several friends or interlocutors about what leading a just life in an ideal, just city would look like. In Plato's dialogue, Socrates first rejects three definitions of justice:

1) Justice is speaking the truth and repaying one's debts.
2) Justice is to benefit one's friends and harm one's enemies.
3) Justice is the advantage of the stronger.[1]

The definition Socrates and his interlocutors finally agree upon states: "justice is doing one's own work and not meddling with what isn't one's own" or "the having and doing of one's own."[2]

The influence of Plato's definition can be seen in our current day understandings of justice. Inherent in this definition is the idea of reward and punishment. Should what is "one's own" be removed from an individual, justice demands that what is "her own" should be returned to her. Furthermore, he who removed the "item" will get what is "his own," "what's coming to him," in some form of punishment. This is "retributive justice" and *seems* to be the kind of justice that the United States is demanding after 9/11.

On September 17, President George W. Bush stated, "We're going to find those evildoers, those barbaric people who attacked our country, and we're going to hold them accountable. We're going to hold the people who house them accountable. The people who think they can provide them safe havens will be held accountable. The people who feed them will be held accountable."[3] On September 21, in his address on terrorism before a joint meeting of Congress he affirmed: "Whether we bring our enemies to justice or bring justice to our enemies, justice will be done." He further stated that "Freedom and fear, justice and cruelty, have always been at war. And we know that God is not neutral between them." Implicit in this last sentence is the idea that God is on the side of freedom and justice and therefore, on the side of the United States and those nations who are with them. For as the president made clear in this same address as well as on many other occasions, "Either you are with us or you are with the terrorists." So, justice and freedom in the form of the United States and its coalition is at war with cruelty and fear, and God is on their side. But what form of justice is warring with cruelty and fear? The question remains unanswered, if it has even been asked.

To return to the platonic roots of the definition, retributive justice attempts to return, in some fashion, that which is "one's own." Its aim is to hold someone accountable for his or her actions or crimes. It is also linked to the idea of holding someone to the social contract. In fact, according to social contract theorists like Thomas Hobbes (1588–1679), retributive justice is the only kind of justice that can work. Hobbes believed that the condition of nature itself was warfare, and that contracts, in the form of laws, whether between individuals or individuals and the state, were the only options for keeping society functioning in any kind of harmony. But holding someone accountable under retributive justice, in order to return to someone what is his own, or inflict some punishment on the criminal if what is one's own has been irretrievably, irrevocably lost or taken away, includes the idea of a criminal trial prior to punishment.

According to Jennifer Llewellyn, retributive justice "has historically seemed to be the most obvious avenue, especially to Western human rights activists or international lawyers, for dispensing justice."[4] Such attempts to dispense justice through criminal trials, be they in local courts or in international courts of law, "respond to the powerful, if not overwhelming, moral intuition that the something that must be done in the wake of gross violations of human rights is that the 'monsters' responsible for the acts in question must be punished."[5] Bush's call to hold accountable those who participated in the attacks, those "barbaric evildoers," monsters indeed, sounds very much like retributive justice. The stated purpose of bombing Afghanistan is to "root the terrorists out of their caves" in order, presumably, to hold them accountable for their actions and punish them in a fitting manner.

And yet, as Arundhati Roy points out, "The UN, reduced now to an ineffective acronym, wasn't even asked to mandate the air strikes. . . . The 'evidence' against the terrorists was shared amongst friends of the 'coalition.' After conferring, they announced that it didn't matter whether or not the 'evidence' would stand up in a court of law. Thus, in an instant, were centuries of jurisprudence carelessly trashed."[6] While retributive justice seems to be at work here, her comment illustrates the fact that a rather central component was, almost from the outset, left out. This component has three parts: first, there has not been a trial to establish guilt or innocence; second, the evidence itself, it is implied, is possibly unconvincing; and third, only friends of the coalition had access to the evidence. In other words, judicial review—on which both the legal system and retributive justice in the United States are based—has been put aside.

There is another concept of justice at work in the discourse, one that is, I believe, being disturbingly and too quickly conflated with retributive justice. In the above quoted speech of September 17, the president also stated the following: "I want justice. . . . And there's an old poster out West . . . I recall, that said 'Wanted, Dead or Alive.'" This same day it was made clear that the assassination order on bin Laden was still in place. This raises many questions, perhaps the most disturbing of which is, what definition of justice includes assassination? Bush was clearly calling to mind the notion of "frontier justice," which conjures up images of the settling of the Wild West. As the introduction from the website of an October 2000 University of Wyoming symposium on "Frontier Justice" states, there were no trials or juries on the frontier—only "the lone lawman standing against desperados, vigilantes, raging battles over rights to land and water, powerful cattle barons and embattled homesteaders."[7] One can almost see the tumbleweed rolling through the streets of Washington, D.C.—only in the current scenario, it's not a movie. And the "good guys" aren't wearing white hats, but battle fatigues and helmets. And we're not even sure if we've found the "bad guys." "We hunt an enemy that hides in shadows and caves," said the president on November 6, and we still don't know where Osama bin Laden is.

"Frontier justice" also conjures up the image of ranchers taking justice into their own hands. The result is that the "official" lawmen often became nothing more than glorified gravediggers. Why would Bush call up such an image? Why would it be used as a rallying cry for justice in the twenty-first century? Frontier justice did not give people a trial in any meaningful sense of the word; it was inherently and undeniably cruel, as the narrative of Elizabeth Roe, who lived on the Texas frontier in the 1870s, illustrates. Her story tells of the ranchers taking matters into their own hands; of one man acting as judge and jury; and of the brutality with which those "judged" guilty were treated: "When my husband's [a Ranger] party went to get the bodies; they found the bodies on the ground, but their heads were still held by the noose of the rope. These bodies had remained until decay had caused the bodies to separate from the heads."[8] Furthermore, there were no coalitions that one could depend on.

Is this why Bush uses the language of frontier justice? Is it a way of keeping in the back of the mind of the other nations joined in the "coalition" to fight terrorism that, as Roy reminds us, "Madeleine Albright once said, '[the United States] will behave multilaterally when we can, and unilaterally when we must'"? Although Secretary of State Colin Powell remarked on October 25 that "[n]obody's called us unilateralist in the past few weeks,"[9] frontier justice may be invoked as a reminder that in the end the United States will take matters into its own hands when it feels fit, for there are questions about how strong the coalition really is, about how long it will last. Are we back to settling a frontier? Is the Middle East the new Wild West?

At the same time that frontier justice is evoked and conflated with retributive justice, there is yet another concept at work behind "justifying" the war—that is, construing it as a "just war." In a November 6 address to an antiterrorism summit in Warsaw, Poland, the president stated that the war on terrorism was "making good progress in a just cause." Just war theory dates back to such thinkers as Augustine (354–430 B.C.E.), Aquinas (1224–74), Suarez (1548–1617), and Grotius (1583–1645) and was originally closely linked to the Christian church. It is studied in military academies and is thus familiar to those running the war. One of its tenets is, not surprisingly, that if war is to be fought, it must be for a "just cause." Yet what constitutes such a cause?

In his 1992 book on the Gulf War, Kenneth Vaux outlines just war ethics, and suggests that George Bush was guided by such a code in his decision to launch the Gulf War. Causes for a just war are outlined as:

*Just cause.* A war can be started only for just reasons. They may include: Vindication of justice, restoring a just international order, protecting innocent life and restoration of human rights.

*Competent authority.* War can be started only by those with responsibility for public order and legitimate authority for engaging the nation in war.

*Comparative justice.* The central question should be: Is the justice of our cause greater than theirs?

*Right intention.* A just war is only a means to gain peace and reconciliation—not humiliation and punishment.

*Last resort.* All nonviolent alternatives should be exhausted.

*Probability of success.* If a successful end is futile, war should not be started.

*Proportionality of projected results.* The good expected from war must be greater than all the foreseen costs.

*Right spirit.* War must be engaged with an attitude of regret.[10]

Can the same be said of "America's New War"? On many counts the current war does seem to uphold several of these tenets. It is stated that the cause is just. On November 9, Bush stated that "We wage a war to save civilization itself. We did not seek it, but we must fight it—and we will prevail." The implication is that the United States and all nations who abhor terrorism have an ethical responsibility, a moral obligation, to join the war—that there is no choice.

Yet behind that assertion is the implication that the war itself is just and necessary for bringing about justice. Analyzing speeches, articles, and press releases, one can see the subtle and, at times, not so subtle argument made that this is a "just war." However, I believe that (at least) three rather significant tenets out of the eight above cannot be reasonably argued for. The three principles that I believe are in question are those of "right intention," "right spirit," and "last resort," which make problematic if not the portrayal of the war as just, then certainly its possibility for bringing about justice.[11]

First, regarding the "right intention" principle, President Bush asserted the following in his November 9 speech: "I have called our military into action to hunt down the members of the al-Qaeda organization who murdered innocent Americans. I gave fair warning to the government that harbors them in Afghanistan. The Taliban made a choice to continue hiding terrorists, and now they are paying a price." This "paying a price" sounds very much like revenge. The repeated use of the word "hunting" cannot be meant but to evoke images of hunting animals and shooting to kill. On November 9 alone, "hunt down the members of the al-Qaeda organization"; "our government has a responsibility to hunt down our enemies—and we will"; November 6, "We hunt an enemy." This image too has overtones of revenge. The earlier references to holding those accountable seems to be for the purpose of punishment; and the call for the assassination of bin Laden cannot in any way be construed on these grounds as anything other than humiliation and punishment. While these dovetail with a concept of retributive justice they cannot, by the above outline of principles, also be part of "right intention" required for a just war.

The "right spirit," that of regret, also seems to be lacking. Again from the White House transcript of the president's November 9 speech: "I'm so proud of our military. (Applause.) Our military is pursuing its mission. We are destroying training camps, disrupting communications, and dismantling air defenses. We are now bombing Taliban front lines. We are deliberately and systematically hunting down these murderers, and we will bring them to justice. (Applause.)" There is no spirit of regret here, rather pride. And when civilians are killed, it is by accident, it is "collateral damage," to be expected in war.

That this war was a means of last resort is also in question. The United States began air strikes on Afghanistan *less than a month* after the September 11 attacks. The president has stated that the United States had no choice but to fight this war. Yet, as Roy pointed out above, there was, at the time the bombings began, as far as we know, no hard evidence as to the guilt of Afghanistan and al-Qaeda. Of course, there is no doubt that the act was an act of terrorism and I am not suggesting that the United States should have "done nothing." But I'm not convinced that enough (any?) other options beyond ultimatums were explored to make what began on October 7 the last resort.

So, without any definition, "justice" has been invoked in at least three forms since the September 11 attacks: "retributive justice," "frontier justice" and the "just" war. The purpose seems clear—invoking the concept of justice shores up support both domestically and internationally. "Justice" compels other nations to join the coalition—for who wants to be on the side of cruelty? Its use also, I believe, guarantees that support for the war will be maintained. Yet no single definition of justice is at work here.

Rather, elements of various definitions of justice that best suit the purpose at the time are selected and then cobbled together under the one term to give the impression that we are all fighting for the same cause—that justice requires, if not demands war, assassination, retribution, punishment, hunting down the enemy, and a little, unavoidable, collateral damage.

We *should* fight for justice. There is no doubt that those responsible for the terrorist acts of September 11 as well as those who have distributed Anthrax should be "brought to justice." But do retributive bombings actually do anything to secure justice— especially for the people of Afghanistan? Is the fact that many Afghan civilians have lost their lives, homes, families, just? Will the bombings return to the victims of the September 11 attacks anything that is "their own"? Does assassination, while it may give some a sense of satisfaction, hold Osama bin Laden accountable for his actions?

One more question must be posed: Have we heard much about peace lately? Perhaps one of the reasons that "peace" together with "justice" has dropped out of the dialogue lately is because to explore all the options for peace would mean that the definition of justice would have to be clarified. On November 9 the president stated that "in the long run, the best way to defend our homeland—the best way to make sure our children can live in peace—is to take the battle to the enemy and to stop them." This assertion that the war is the best way to ensure peace should be questioned. As Roy points out: "When he announced the air strikes, President George Bush said: 'We're a peaceful nation.' America's favourite ambassador, Tony Blair, (who also holds the portfolio of prime minister of the UK), echoed him: 'We're a peaceful people.' So now we know. Pigs are horses. Girls are boys. War is peace."[12]

When considering retributive justice, one central issue must be acknowledged: it is entirely possible that the cycle of retribution will not stop. If we look at what we know of the terrorists' motive for the September 11 attacks, we see that, for them, the attack was an act of retribution. The United States and its coalition are in turn retaliating, attempting to gain retribution. Countless examples around the globe, such as the conflict between Israel and Palestine, demonstrate that it is a very real possibility that the cycle of violence may not end but may in fact escalate. The cycle of retribution only destroys increasing numbers of individuals, families, communities—to say nothing of opportunities for fostering peace.

There is at least one definition of justice that cannot be used to "justify" the current war, but that does foster peace: restorative justice. This kind of justice has not had a voice in the discourse. If one attempts to propose nonviolent, pacifist options for dealing with the tragedy, accusations fly: "So you are suggesting that we just do nothing??!" The following exchange between CNN's Rosemary Church and the Dalai Lama regarding 9/11 is a perfect illustration of what is often the immediate answer to suggestions of nonviolent responses:

> *Church:* How do you think the United States should respond?
> *Dalai Lama:* This is a very difficult question, but basically I feel when you take counter-measures for violence, you need to very carefully think, and use human wisdom according to a non-violent principle. I think this is very important. This is my feeling.
> *Church:* What message do you think that sends the world if the U.S., as a superpower, sits back and accepts these kinds of terrorist attacks and does nothing?[13]

As we see from the above exchange, "pacifism" gets conflated with "passivism" and the dialogue is all but shut down. Such an attitude trivializes nonviolent responses and leaves no room for this voice in the current dialogue. What the Dalai Lama and those concerned with fostering peace are proposing is not "doing nothing." There is a theory of justice that is a nonviolent response—restorative justice. Most recently implemented in South Africa, restorative justice is usually put into place after a conflict, as a way to deal with the past and distribute justice. Clearly the conflict provoked by the events of September 11 is not yet in the past, and it seems that it will be a long time before it will be in the past. However, restorative justice provides us with a framework to truly unite the resolve for peace—if that, indeed, is the objective.

Restorative justice requires us to focus on the victims, but also widens the scope to include the offender and the communities in which both live. A space between, a space of dialogue, is opened up. Restorative justice is "relational" but it does not do away with notions of accountability or responsibility. Rather than demonizing or "enemizing" the other, it demands that we recognize the "enemy's" humanity. Restorative justice attempts to heal, and to repair relationships and harm done to the victims. Once we start to explore this alternative definition of justice in this context we see that it is extremely demanding—the victim and the community are called upon to "humanize" the enemy, and the same demand is made upon the enemy and his or her community. I do not know how, exactly, we could employ restorative justice in the current situation, how we could get the U.S. government and its coalition to have a dialogue with Osama bin Laden and the Taliban and vice versa. What I do know is that asking us to recognize the humanity of the "enemy," asking the "enemy" to listen to the victim, and asking us to enter into a true dialogue brings the innocent victims on all sides to the forefront and serves to unite all of humankind, not just those who live in the United States.

After 9/11, citizens of the United States have something in common with *all* victims of terrorism around the world, and *this* bond, whether one lives in the United States or Rwanda or Bosnia, *this* is the power that can be harnessed to foster peace in the world. Restorative justice recognizes the complexities of a situation—it requires that, rather than backing into a corner, we step into a space of dialogue and recognize that framing the conflict in terms of "good versus evil," "light versus darkness," "freedom versus fear," "justice versus cruelty," does not serve to restore peace, but to justify war.

**NOTES**

1. Plato, *Republic*, trans. G. M. A. Grube (Indianapolis: Hackett, 1992), 331b–354c.

2. Ibid., 433b, 433e–434a.

3. "Bush: bin Laden 'Prime Suspect,'" CNN.com, September 17, 2001 (http://www.cnn.com/2001/US/09/17/bush.powell.terrorism/index.html).

4. Jennifer Llewellyn, "Justice for South Africa: Restorative Justice and the South African Truth and Reconciliation Commission," in *Moral Issues in Global Perspective*, ed. Christine Koggel (Peterborough, Canada: Broadview Press, 1999), 100.

5. Ibid., 101.

6. Arundhati Roy, "Brutality Smeared in Peanut Butter: Why America Must Stop the War Now," *Guardian*, October 23, 2001.

7. Frontier Justice Symposium, Buffalo Bill Historical Center, October 19–21, 2000 (http://www.bbhc.org/edu/fjs2000_01.html).

8. "Frontier Justice," American Memory Timeline, U.S. Library of Congress (http://memory.loc.gov/ammem/ndlpedu/features/timeline/riseind/west/justice.html).

9. Marcus Gee, "World Watch," *The Globe and Mail*, October 25, 2001: A2.

10. Kenneth L. Vaux, *Ethics and the Gulf War: Religion, Rhetoric and Righteousness* (Boulder: Westview Press, 1992), 88–89.

11. It is also interesting to note that "justice" is part of the definition of what constitutes a just war—once again without definition.

12. Roy, "Brutality Smeared in Peanut Butter."

13. "Dalai Lama to U.S.: Use 'Human Wisdom,'" CNN.com, September 20, 2001 (http://www.cnn.com/2001/WORLD/asiapcf/south/09/20/ret.dalai.lama/index.html)

## SUGGESTIONS FOR FURTHER READING

Aristotle. *Nichomachean Ethics* (ca. mid-fourth century B.C.). Translated by D. Ross, revised J. L. Ackrill and J. O. Urmson. Oxford: Oxford University Press, 1980.

Hobbes, T. *Leviathan* (1651). Edited by R. Tuck. Cambridge: Cambridge University Press, 1991.

Kymlicka, W. *Contemporary Political Philosophy: An Introduction.* Oxford: Clarendon Press, 1990.

Rotberg, Robert I., and Dennis Thompson, eds. *Truth v. Justice: The Morality of Truth Commissions.* Princeton: Princeton University Press, 2000.

Strang, Heather, and John Braithwaite, eds. *Restorative Justice and Civil Society.* Cambridge: Cambridge University Press, 2001.

Tutu, Desmond. *No Future without Forgiveness.* New York: Doubleday, 1999.

# 10. Targets

Philip T. Neisser

War is verbal as well as physical, as each side speaks of the other side in ways that, to one degree or another, reduce them to abstractions, or demonize them, or both. Such talk always has its direct wartime meaning and purpose, but also makes broader claims, typically justifications of the way of life, or of the dominant, elite perspective, of each side. The term looked at closely in this essay is "targets," as it is deployed in the war talk created by the United States in its conflict with the Afghan Taliban and al-Qaeda.

People use terms like "targets" in part because their fundamental human compassion leads them to seek a way to distance themselves, or look away, from raw violence. There are many context-specific factors, however, that shape today's war talk, factors less savory than compassion. These include identities encouraged by military training; theories of international relations which map the world in highly abstract terms and which see world stability and order as a function of force; and the drive of the corporate state, an entity that maps the world in abstract terms as so many consumers, as zones of "labor flexibility," as "emerging markets," as areas of potential "profitability," and so on. Given the power of the contemporary corporate state, and given that in much of today's warfare killing is highly technologically mediated and that those who kill are in several ways at a distance from the event, it is not surprising that contemporary war talk tends to lean heavily on abstraction. This is all the more the case when aerial bombing is the main means of attack, as it has been so far in the U.S. campaign against the Taliban regime and the al-Qaeda network in Afghanistan. Thus much of the U.S. war reporting and official information is about "targets." Bombs are aimed at "military targets," "installations" are "targeted," "civilian targets" are not being aimed at, and so on.

The term "targets" helps speaker and audience alike to see the war in abstract terms. By abstraction I mean the representation of particular aspects of reality in terms that refer to universal categories in which the particulars can be subsumed. Abstraction can also be defined as representations that accomplish the near disappearance of particular facts except insofar as they take their place in a theory about how the particulars fit together in a larger whole. Examples of abstraction include when the death of a person is rendered only in a statistic that summarizes casualties in general, or when unemployed workers appear in language only as a force that keeps inflation at a reasonable level.

Abstraction is never simply the result of the use of a particular term. Rather it is an effect terms have, often multiple and/or unintended, when deployed in a certain factual and terminological context. Nonetheless, "targets," along with its partner or substitute, "positions," has been a pivotal term in U.S. descriptions of the war. Its constant use helps make the killing and destruction of bombing disappear as such, only to reappear as mere advances or setbacks in the movement of the "campaign" toward its various "objectives," such as peace, stability, and an end to terrorism. Sentences like the following are typical. "In the most extensive effort of the bombing campaign so far, U.S. bombers struck a series of Taliban targets today." Or "The Pentagon announced today that attacks on military targets have significantly eroded the anti-aircraft capacity of the Taliban regime." Sometimes goals and attacks are explicitly linked: "in the second week of the U.S.–led war against terrorism, planes bombarded targets in the North of Afghanistan."

Crucial to the deployment of the word "targets" is the differentiation made between "military" and "civilian" targets. This distinction, which forms such a central part of treaty-based attempts to limit the scope of modern warfare, easily slides in practice into dishonesty about killing or, more ominously, into a means to dehumanize or "disappear" entire groups of people, as if soldiers don't die, or aren't truly people while being soldiers. This dehumanization runs throughout the press releases, speeches, and press coverage of the war, as humans become "military targets" or "Taliban positions," and the goals are a "transition government," "an end to terrorism," and the like, rather than killing and terrorizing a group of people.

The rendering of people or of infrastructure as targets works, in concert with other phrases, to encourage a grasp of the meaning of the war as if were—despite obvious, and regrettable, violent facts—essentially a large-scale nonviolent exercise, maybe even a kind of grand organized effort to tackle a social problem, sort of like a new "war on poverty." (It is said, after all, that the war on terrorism is a multifaceted struggle that includes diplomatic and economic projects, such as massive food drops in the Afghan countryside.) Things might appear quite different if, say, news reports said, "roads and bridges people need to get to work and to get food were once again bombed today," or if reporters said, "more Afghans lost members of their families today, as U.S. planes pounded bases where young soldiers, just doing what is expected of them, or fighting for their country, are stationed."

A particularly remarkable example of the abstraction accomplished by the language of "targets" appeared in the *Chicago Sun-Times* of Saturday, October 20, 2001.

Late Friday, the Pentagon reported that a U.S. helicopter supporting a commando raid in Afghanistan crashed in neighboring Pakistan, killing two people in the first combat-related
American deaths of the military campaign. (p. 2)

The facts here are fairly straightforward, though the text does include the word "campaign," an old military word become an
election word, then perhaps returned to the military context in
ways that help some see the war as an essentially benign project.
A bit further on in the article the deaths in the crash reappear in
a new and remarkable way:

The deaths bring to three the number of people killed since
the U.S. military campaign against the al-Qaida terror network
and the Taliban began October 7th. Master Sgt. Evander An-
drews . . . was killed last week in a forklift accident while building an airstrip in Qatar. (p. 2)

The missing deaths in this passage are striking. The U.S. government had, prior to the helicopter crash, been bombing
Afghanistan for almost two weeks. Of course many people were
killed. How could someone experience the American deaths as
the first deaths? And how could that person's words find their way
unedited into a lead story of the "America Fights Back" coverage?
     The *Sun-Times* words are not the result of any "plot" behind
the scenes to propagandize the public or sell war. Nor is the general production of euphemism, rationalization, and distortion
strictly speaking anything like the result of a plan to fool the public. It is true that the government (or different, imperfectly co-
ordinated elements of government) self-consciously crafts a public relations effort during each war, and as the years go by the so-
phistication of such efforts has grown. It is also true that since
the Vietnam public relations "disaster" (this is how many foreign

relations analysts have grasped the loss in Vietnam, as if democracy at home was the problem), special attention has been paid to the issue of the reporting of casualties. But, as any good salesperson knows, you've got to believe in your product, and those working to present the war to the public are surely thinking (and maybe even dreaming) in the same morally neutralizing terms which they offer to their audience. This is not because they too have been duped by some smaller, more secret group of power holders, so much as it is because journalists, governmental spokespersons, the president, congresspersons, and the big business elite are like the rest of us in that they are searching for concepts to help them feel that they know what is going on and which enable them to feel as if they are responding in a morally coherent fashion. They also feel the pressures, and fall into the traditions, of their role within an institution. "Doublethink" and "newspeak" (terms from George Orwell's *1984*) are thus not so much foisted on one group by another as a way people fool themselves, a spell cast by discourse. And of course, once started, doublethink takes on a life of its own.

If not the result of a plot, why then did a bit of newspeak slip into the *Chicago Sun-Times?* A likely reason is the regular press and news conference rendering of bombing raids in abstract, strategic terms as efforts aimed at "targets" and "positions." This language helps see to it that the deaths caused when U.S. attacks hit their targets get subsumed under the heading of mere war data, or are not even noticed as such, much less counted or otherwise brought up. Thus the deaths of the helicopter occupants and the forklift operator seemed like the first ones to many of those looking at events from a U.S. point of view. When enemy deaths do reach the threshold of attention, it is usually in indirect and abstract terms, for example in relation to a discussion of the goals of the U.S. effort, or of the strategy being followed to reach those goals. For example, on National Public Radio at one point it was announced that "Taliban soldiers were bombed earlier today," as part of "Northern Alliance efforts to gain control" over a "strategic city."

Civilian deaths are another matter. U.S. officials, reporters, and commentators have regularly expressed great concern about the need to avoid civilian loss of life. When some Red Cross warehouses were accidentally bombed by U.S. warplanes, and several humanitarian workers were killed, the events were discussed again and again, with great attention to detail, in ways that made clear the moral unacceptability of aiming at civilian targets (as well as the moral acceptability of doing so if it happens accidentally and as part of a just war effort). And when the United States was charged by Taliban officials with causing many other civilian deaths, and reporters were guided to the sites of alleged attacks, the U.S. government again made clear its commitment to avoid such incidents. The United States denied the validity of some claims, pointed out that others are yet unconfirmed, and in a few cases acknowledged that errors were made and civilians were indeed, regretfully, bombed. Finally, the U.S. government has in turn made allegations of its own, saying that the Taliban military has purposefully placed many of their troops and military hardware in civilian areas. In all this back and forth exchange about what has taken place, one consistent message comes through— the moral unacceptability of military actions aimed at civilians.

There are good, humanitarian reasons for making a distinction between civilian and military targets, but the effect of all the expressions of concern over civilian loss of life is nonetheless not as benevolent as it first appears. This is for at least four reasons. First, the very concern about civilian life makes the lives of soldiers and military support personnel seem like something not worthy of concern. In the case of the bombings of the Red Cross, individuals from around the world—UN officials and Red Cross officials, for example—were quoted voicing their insistence that civilian loss of life must be scrupulously avoided. In the meantime, reporting on the number of "successful" bombing raids continued, with no attention whatsoever to the details and no expressions of moral concern.

Second, the talk of the great importance of avoiding killing civilians helps cement the convenient myth that the destruction of military targets does not hurt civilians. This is not true, first of all because nonmilitary persons are of course killed or injured by attacks aimed at the military, even when the bombs are on target and the target is well chosen. Moreover, targets considered "military" might be gas pipelines, water treatment plants, bridges, and the like; all things that civilians may depend on for their very lives. It is true that, as this essay goes to press, it is not clear that the United States has been attacking such targets in Afghanistan, but it is also true that very little information has been provided about what exactly is being attacked, and very little concern over gathering this information has been shown by the press. This is despite the precedent set by the U.S.-Iraq war a decade ago, when the United States destroyed much Iraqi infrastructure (water treatment plants, water pipelines, and so on) in ways that have contributed to the impoverishment, desperation, disease, and death of thousands of civilians.

Third, and paradoxically, the killing of civilians is in some ways made easier by all the talk of the need to avoid killing them. One reason for this is that concern is directed away from the civilians as dead individuals and toward such things as the issue of "correct" or "successful" targeting (it is said to be difficult in wartime) and at the intentions of those who target (it is noted that the important thing is that bombers did not intend to strike civilians, and thus, it is implied, the bombers and their government are still morally superior to the enemy, despite the accident). Civilian-target talk can, then, function as ritualistic demonstrations of concern, making it easier for the news audience to accept civilian deaths, and in turn making it easier for the U.S. military to cause such deaths.

Fourth, the focus on civilian deaths is a public relations opportunity for the U.S. government, as it is able to stress its care for the health and well-being of peoples all over the world. This message, sent also by means of issuance of, and the talk of, "humanitarian aid," helps to obscure the fact that U.S. government policies and programs have for decades been leading the way in imposing a radical right wing, ultra-free market, neoliberal version of globalization onto developing nations. This version of globalization, under way since at least the Reagan and Thatcher years, is a patent failure when it comes to its stated goals of reducing poverty and creating widespread growth and improved social welfare. Instead, unprecedented growth has brought with it increased inequality, poverty, and desperation. It has brought the health-threatening proliferation of corporate-chain-produced processed food, damage to the world's topsoil and rainforests, the spreading of toxins deeper into the food chain, and the erosion of job security and wage security for middle classes in developing nations.

It is important to repeat that the civilian-military distinction is by no means an entirely bad idea, or one that can be simply dispensed with. It clearly has the potential to restrict the scope of warfare. Is it playing that role to some extent in the U.S.-Taliban conflict? Maybe, thanks to the targeting of the military, the people killed and maimed by U.S. attacks are more likely to be actual aggressors against U.S. forces. Maybe they are also a little more likely to endorse the attacks that took place against the United States, and so in some sense to be more "deserving." Maybe also they have the option to desert and change sides. If so, then maybe the distinction has a moral foundation and a useful purpose.

Some might argue as well that the military-civilian distinction will help end the Afghan conflict sooner rather than later. Military targets are those that by definition (at least supposedly) enhance the military power of the other side, and so their destruction may hasten surrender, or otherwise reduce death, as for example if troops or hardware that would have been used aggressively are rendered useless through death and destruction.

Another possible argument in favor of a military-civilian distinction is that it expresses the principle of regret for loss of life, by means of its assertion that aggression should be limited to attacks on those who are themselves aggressors. The key idea here is that military personnel in wartime represent the states for which they fight, and thus represent aggression in ways that civilians do not. Thus each side should draw a line between the military and the civilians.

On the other hand, the positive aspects of the military-civilian distinction may be more theoretical than real. In practice, many soldiers have little or no choice but to enlist, are very limited in their sources of information (which may make any endorsement by them of attacks on the United States relatively reasonable or understandable), and may need military pay to feed themselves and their families. And, in an ultimate sense, the lives of soldiers—any soldiers—are just as real and just as sacred as the lives of civilians. In wartime each side works hard to forget this fact, and this forgetting is, as was said above, made easier by all the concern expressed about the value of civilian lives. When it comes to the idea that attacking the right targets may end the war sooner, this may be true, but it does not mean that the war is ended sooner by speaking as if the destruction of military, rather than civilian, targets is less morally problematic. And, finally, the notion that military personnel represent the state for which they fight is highly questionable.

This notion that troops "represent" states goes back a long way. Aquinas, for example, alludes to the idea when he lays down the conditions for a just war: it must be fought under the auspices of a public authority with a right to mobilize the people; it must be fought for a cause that is just, meaning that those under attack must have committed an offense deserving of a response; and it must be carried out with right intention *(Summa Theologiae,* II–II, qu. 40). The second condition seems at least to imply that in a war opposing combatants are in part somehow responsible for the offenses committed by the nation-state for which they fight. It may also, then, be read to imply that special restraint should be exercised when it comes to attacks on "civilians." Rousseau, in *The Social Contract* (I, IV), makes the civilian-military distinction quite clear:

> The object of the war being destruction of a hostile state, the other side has a right to kill its defenders, while they are bearing arms; but as soon as they lay them down and surrender, they cease to be enemies or instruments of the enemy, and become once again merely men, whose life no one has any right to take.

Rousseau speaks to counsel restraint, but he nonetheless implies that those who bear arms are not "merely men." Instead they represent a "hostile state"; they are the enemy, apparently both more than and different than "men." Military lives are, as it were, representatives of a "side." Is this not a morally unacceptable way to speak of human beings? Doesn't this way of speaking reveal the obvious dangers of just war theory, that it will be used to justify wars that are not in fact just? For the prosecutors of a war, whether just or unjust in its aims, the idea that enemy soldiers are mere extensions of a state or a ruler is quite convenient. In the U.S.-Afghan context, the discourse of the "enemy" as a unified "side" is directly linked to the language that describes attacks on "targets" and "positions" as mere parts of an overall action against an enemy state. All the terms are linked in a web of abstraction, and attention is deflected away from the moral questions raised by attacks on human beings.

The language of targets thus helps move the actions of war into the realm of the abstract; it objectifies human life. And military targets become more abstract and more objectified each and every time the importance of avoiding civilian casualties is mentioned, at least if no acknowledgment comes at the same time of a need to be concerned about military lives as well. Slowly, step by step, U.S. observers are inured to the obvious and awful loss of life taking place. The status and situation of the typical enemy soldier becomes less and less visible to these observers. This process, as was said above, is driven by the desire to manage compassion, by warrior ethics, by theories of international relations, and by the imperatives of the modern state. It is important that we look in more detail at the last two of these forces, as they have particular relevance in the contemporary period.

Today's objectification of life finds some of its roots in what might best be termed the "drive of the corporate state." Today's state is a constellation of interlocked, institutionally situated, powerful actors, actors whose power is highly constrained by their institutional roles, by culture, and by politics. Despite what the anti–big government types say, the state in the United States today is not just the government (in fact a more democratic government and a more organized and politicized populace is badly needed to counter the power of today's state). The state is, rather, a semimerged combination of the biggest corporations, finance companies, and banks, along with key financial, economic, and military parts of the government. This state includes "advisory groups" that form close working relationships with top government officials. It also includes the major government contractors (such as Lockheed Martin), numerous think tanks (such as the Rand Corporation) and, increasingly, the global treaty organizations (such as the World Trade Organization) that largely bypass democracy in the name of enforcing "free trade." And the state also includes—in a looser, less reliable way—schools, police forces, D.A.R.E. programs, corporate owned media companies, and the like.

These groups are only "semimerged" in that the connections between them are partial, and also in that they are not engaged in a systematic, well-thought out, or conscious plan to rule. There is no conspiracy. But all the groups are alike in that they are instruments of power, action, and culture, and running in so many ways through all of them is a single thread: a commitment to an economic outlook on the world that prioritizes supporting the current system of investment, profit, and growth, and that sees truly active, unpredictable citizens as a hindrance. True, the corporate state is divided along the lines of "liberal" and "conservative" alike when it comes to "social issues" such as abortion rights or school prayer. True also, the corporate state does contain potentially rebellious elements, and work is required to keep the coalition together. But social issues and other differences are not generally allowed to stand in the way of the main thrust of the state as such, which is its drive to expand its own power, to secure predictable and profitable investment scenarios for global capital, and to secure predictable relationships with other states. These are the imperatives of the state today, and they do much to shape, in a mostly unconscious or good-intentioned way, the production of wartime terminology.

One especially relevant segment of the state, when it comes to wartime terminology, is what is often called "the foreign policy establishment." This is a loosely conglomerated source of experts, theories, and strategic planning, with elements both inside and outside government. The model of security which is institutionalized in this establishment (despite the existence of competing perspectives in academic discourse) is partly a result of the imperatives of state, and partly an accident of history, as certain foreign policy theories have, despite blind spots and false assumptions, become entrenched in the very language of "foreign affairs." According to these theories (sometimes misleadingly labeled "realist"), national security requires manipulation of the relationship between nation-states so as to create a favorable and stable balance of power. This balance of power then goes by the name of "stability" in general, a state-centered view of the world which overlooks the issue of what counts as "stability" or "security" in life for individuals.

How does the state-centered model of security connect to the term "targets"? To start with, the model itself is rife with such language. To be trained in foreign policy analysis is to be schooled to see the world in abstract terms, as a set of nation-states to be played off each other, as a kind of dance of force. In the name of the goal of a stable and favorable balance of power, it is occasionally deemed necessary to attack various "targets." Instability is visited upon actual human lives, but appears in description to be a movement toward stability.

In the dominant state-centered worldview of today's foreign policy, justice, while not dismissed per se, nonetheless tends to disappear from the security equation. Justice, for example, was not the issue when the U.S. government decided it should arm Saddam Hussein in Iraq so as to balance the power of Iran. Justice is not the issue as the United States mostly overlooks the brutal Turkish oppression of Kurds and their culture by the Turkish government. Nor do U.S. strategic planners seem to consider a just Afghanistan as the key to a successful and appropriate response to the attacks on the United States of September 11. While the U.S. government has expressed concern about the fact that its Afghan ally against the Taliban, the Northern Alliance, is possibly more brutal in its ways than the Taliban itself, this concern tends to take the form of worry over what sort of alliance could reliably control a post-Taliban Afghanistan and remain allied to the United States. Thus the discourse directs attention away from justice in itself, leaving the least room for any long-term thinking about justice. It is hard to imagine, for example, foreign policy analysts stressing the need to reconfigure IMF and World Bank policies in West Asia and in the world. Ideas such as these, if they come up at all, are treated as separate "ethical" or "economic" issues.

The failure to consider justice as part and parcel of safety and security is thought of by many to be hard-headed realism, but it is not. It is a flawed way to think about power, long-term global stability, and military strategy. Terrorist Kurdish rebels would, for example, be hard-pressed to get recruits if it wasn't for the suppression of the Kurds. And maybe the best way for the United States to fight the Taliban is to prioritize developing economies in West Asia and around the world that provide basic needs for the common people, even if this cuts into the power of corporations to seek profits and expansion.

The failure to properly consider justice is not, however, merely a mistake. Instead, it is in keeping with the imperatives of the contemporary state. These imperatives, in part through the medium of the foreign policy establishment, help to explain the U.S. government's penchant for forming alliances with regimes with horrific human rights records. This practice is not simply a leftover of the Cold War, nor was it ever motivated simply and solely by the Soviet threat. Rather the general guiding principle is the notion that provision must be made for the expansion of the reach of big investors around the world, on terms favorable to the most profit. Nations that provide that access are typically welcomed as allies. Vehicles for creating this access include NAFTA, NATO, the World Bank, the IMF, the WTO, and other alliances of big business-oriented elites, scholars, and government officials.

Another vehicle for crafting a world safe for fast profits is war. War is a calamity, but from an abstract, global perspective it is an opportunity. Given the nature of the U.S. state, and given the sorry state of democratic discourse in the United States, the U.S. government will likely continue to follow familiar patterns in its dealings with Afghanistan. This will mean priorities such as "balancing" the power of China with an Afghan ally, however brutal, or crafting an Afghan regime that agrees to build a pipeline through its territory. Ideas that promise real prosperity for ordinary Afghan people will most likely not receive serious consideration. The United States is likely, in other words, to pursue policies that in the long run make its own people less safe and secure, even though the impetus will have been a "war against terrorism." And this will have been made possible in part by the spell woven by the language of "targets."

One irony of the situation is that many in the United States who have adamantly refused to objectify the deaths caused by the World Trade Center attack (one person said, "five thousand people didn't die here; five thousand individuals died") have nonetheless helped to objectify the lives of others: members of al-Qaeda, the Taliban, and the Afghan military, people who work at or near Afghan military installations, and even people who play various civilian roles. Another irony is that a real concern to minimize the loss of civilian life through accurate "targeting" has helped to justify a war effort which is itself shaped by imperatives of a corporate state which "targets" civilians around the world for economic insecurity or, in the case of some, for death from toxic forms of economic development or from the easily treated diseases of poverty and a poor water supply. In part because of the laserlike focus, created by the war, on the importance of protecting people from terrorist force, the current global system has come to appear as if it is a humanitarian force, as the opposite of "terrorism." Legitimate questions about the harm it does to people recede into the background, or worse, are seen as catering to the enemy. Thus it becomes politically that much harder for people to "target" the global policies of the modern corporate state.

In conclusion, it's a small step from our society's dominant procorporate principles of national security to seeing military targets as something other than flesh and blood. After all, no flesh and blood appears on the strategic maps which are on the walls of planning rooms and in the minds of the planners. And no flesh and blood appears in the models of economists concerning the parameters for growth in the next quarter.

What can be done? As individuals, we can each make an effort to pick blunt words which challenge ourselves morally, and which challenge the current doublespeak. We can be attuned to shifts in the meanings of phrases, think about what is implied when people speak, and consciously decide where we stand and how we should talk. We can avoid making personal judgments about the integrity of the people whose pronouncements offend us, instead working to offer another perspective. And we can strive to target structures, such as the "free trade" system of the emerging global economy, along with their allied abstractions, such as "stability," in the name of life, instead of targeting life in the name of structures and abstractions.

## SUGGESTIONS FOR FURTHER READING

Danaher, Kevin, ed. *Democratizing the Global Economy: The Battle against the World Bank and the IMF.* Monroe, Maine: Common Courage Press, 2001.

Der Derian, James, and Michael J. Shapiro, eds. *International/Intertextual Relations: Postmodern Readings of World Politics.* Lexington, Mass.: Lexington Books, 1989.

Domhoff, G. William. *The Power Elite and the State: How Policy Is Made in America.* New York: Aldine de Gruyter, 1990.

Frank, Ellen et al., eds. *Real World Globalization,* 6th ed. Cambridge, Mass.: The Dollars and Sense Collective, 2000.

Wolin, Sheldon. *The Presence of the Past: Essays on the State and the Constitution.* Baltimore: Johns Hopkins University Press, 1989.

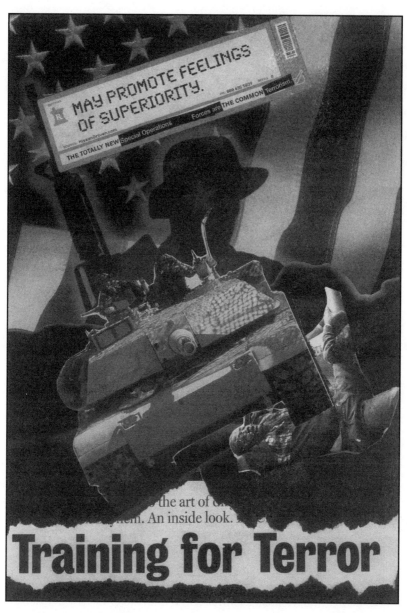

Ross Glover, *Common Terrorism*. Reprinted with the permission of Ross Glover.

# 11. Terrorism

JOHN COLLINS

A scenario: The U.S. government identifies an Arab as the man responsible for a particular act of political violence, then initiates a retaliatory bombing campaign in the Middle East, generating a wave of patriotic sentiment and xenophobia from Maine to Hawaii. The airwaves are filled with the voices of "terrorism experts" and retired military officers who speak gravely about the need to respond forcefully to "the terrorists." Almost overnight, public opinion polls indicate near-universal support for the notion that "terrorism" is now the country's number one problem. Strangely, actual definitions of "terrorism" are nowhere to be found. Meanwhile, in the pages of the alternative press, voices of dissent also begin to appear. One article reads as follows:

> Past and future bombing raids aside, the terrorism craze is dangerous because it consolidates the immense, unrestrained pseudopatriotic narcissism we are nourishing. Is there no limit to the folly that convinces large numbers of Americans that it is now unsafe to travel, and at the same time blinds them to all the pain and violence that so many people in Africa, Asia and Latin America must endure simply because we have decided that local oppressors . . . can go on with their killing . . . ? Is there no way to participate in politics beyond the repetition of

prefabricated slogans? What happened to the precision, discrimination and critical humanism that we celebrate as the
hallmarks of liberal education and the Western heritage?[1]

A "terrorism craze" . . . a rash of "pseudopatriotic narcissism" . . .
blindness to the suffering of others . . . public discussion marked
by the "repetition of prefabricated slogans"—these are defining
characteristics of American society after September 11, 2001. Yet
the passage I have just quoted comes not from 2001—nor, for
that matter, from the Gulf War of 1991—but rather from an article written by Edward Said in 1986 in the aftermath of the U.S.
bombing of Libya. In reviewing future Israeli Prime Minister
Benjamin Netanyahu's book *Terrorism: How the West Can Win,* Said
argued forcefully that the very notion of "terrorism" needed to
be questioned because of its vagueness and because of the way it
was being used in the 1980s by policy makers in the United
States, Israel, and elsewhere as a label for their political enemies.
Looking at the present, post–September 11 situation, one is
tempted to conclude that Said's important observations are now
as forgotten as the bombing of Libya and the brief period when
Muammar Qaddafi provided the bridge between Ayatollah
Khomeini and Saddam Hussein as the U.S. government's Middle
Eastern demon of choice.

The bombing of Libya, however, is but one chapter in a long
story. Across the globe, memories of invasions, proxy wars, covert
destabilization campaigns, coups, bombing campaigns, and
other military interventions by the United States and its allies
loom large in the collective consciousness of entire populations
who have good reason to be skeptical when the U.S. government
proclaims itself to be taking the moral high ground and leading
a global "war on terrorism." Americans, on the other hand, are
often unaware of the darker chapters in the history of their nation's foreign policy. How many remember the CIA-backed overthrow of Iran's government in 1953? Or the support the United

States gave to the murderous Renamo movement in Mozambique during the 1980s in the name of anticommunism? Or, even more recently, Israel's use of American-made shells to bomb a United Nations peacekeeping base at Qana, Lebanon, in 1996, an action that killed 102 civilians and drew no significant condemnation from Washington? Any attempt to grapple with "terrorism," then, must also address the particular forms of collective amnesia that have marked the relationship between the United States and the so-called "Third World" during the second half of the twentieth century. It is this amnesia that allows Americans to act surprised when confronted with those whose recollections of violence are considerably more vivid and less selective.

Equally important for the purposes of this essay, the same amnesia has the effect of hiding the history of "terrorism" as a concept, specifically the ways in which the meaning of the term was shaped in recent decades by individuals with close links to American power. What we think we "know" about "terrorism" is not an objective reality; on the contrary, the very idea of "terrorism" is the product of specific efforts by specific people to define certain examples of political violence (typically violence committed by those who are opposed to U.S. policies in the world) as illegitimate. In other words, when someone uses the word "terrorism," they are describing the world in a way that works to the advantage of the powerful. In cultural studies, the academic field in which I was trained, words and ideas that masquerade as neutral or objective "reality," while actually expressing the narrow interests of a dominant group, are called *ideology*. We can say that ideology is most successful when it is able to erase its own footprints, that is, when people are not aware of the work that had to be done in order to fix the meaning of the word or idea in question. The concept of "terrorism," in this sense, appears to be a very effective example of ideology because the public at large has come to accept the definition promoted by the U.S. political elite, without knowing how this definition was created

in the first place. Yet even this explanation is unsatisfactory because, for reasons I will discuss below, U.S. officials actually have
rarely provided explicit definitions of "terrorism," relying instead on a vague, even tautological set of descriptions and assumptions that mask the government's own historical role in
carrying out, supporting, and provoking political violence.
Thus we have a situation in which Americans are being asked to
support an open-ended war not against a clearly defined
"enemy," but rather against an ideological concept whose definition is assumed rather than offered.

In this light, I argue that the obvious and important question
now being asked by critically minded citizens (What, exactly, is
"terrorism"?) needs to be modified to take into account the
process through which the concept of "terrorism" was *made understandable* to Americans. The question then becomes, What is
"terrorism" such that we can declare war on it?

## The Invention of "Terrorism"

In its earliest usage, the concept of "terrorism" surfaced in the aftermath of the French revolution, when the nation's new leaders
employed a "reign of terror" to eliminate their political enemies
and consolidate their hold on power. We also know that nineteenth-century Russian revolutionaries were labeled "terrorists"
because they used violence to pursue their political ends. As late
as 1965, the word "terrorism" had not entered into popular usage
in the United States. Scarcely a decade later, however, the term
had acquired a very specific set of meanings, and ordinary citizens understood political leaders who invoked "terrorism" as a
"threat." How did this change happen?

On an immediate level, the emergence of "terrorism" as a subject of political concern can be traced to a series of high-profile

kidnappings and skyjackings carried out by radical groups rang-
ing from the Popular Front for the Liberation of Palestine
(PFLP) to the Japanese Red Army in the early 1970s. By this time,
however, the wave of anticolonial insurrections in the decades
following World War II had already led analysts and policy makers to speak of new types of warfare waged by "terrorists" and
"urban guerrillas." Into this picture we must add the domestic social unrest of the late 1960s, when students and other Americans
began to use increasingly confrontational tactics to protest the
U.S. war in Vietnam, the effects of racism and police brutality,
and the consolidation of a capitalist system rooted in consumerism, patriarchy, militarism, rampant individualism, and environmental unsustainability. Understanding this larger context
helps explain why the idea of "terrorism" would be so attractive
to those members of the U.S. political and intellectual elite who
concerned themselves with defining the nation's foreign and defense policy agendas. It is these people, working at the intersections of major institutions (government, academy, military,
media), who are responsible for the invention of "terrorism" as
an object of public policy, military action, and intense, sometimes hysterical public obsession.

The creation of structures within the U.S. government to deal
with "terrorism" may be traced to the late 1960s, when Richard
Nixon used a "law and order" platform to win the White House on
the heels of the turbulent summer of 1968. The efforts of the
Nixon Administration to expand the monitoring and disruption
(sometimes through assassination) of domestic political opponents are legendary; many of these actions were exposed in the
hearings of the 1975 Select Committee to Study Governmental
Operations with Respect to Intelligence Activities (popularly
known as the Church Committee after its chairman, Senator
Frank Church). Nixon was also responsible for creating the Cabinet Committee to Combat Terrorism in 1972, and for appointing

a special assistant to the Secretary of State to deal with "terrorism." The short-lived Ford Administration brought little change in policy, other than dismantling some domestic surveillance operations in the wake of the Watergate scandal and continuing the established "no negotiations" policy of dealing with "terrorist" demands. The Carter Administration, however, took a range of streamlining measures, including the creation of several important structures: the Special Coordination Committee (SCC) of the National Security Council, designed to handle crisis management issues at the highest level; the Executive Committee on Terrorism (ECT), under the SCC, consisting of representatives from the CIA, NSC, and the Departments of State, Defense, Justice, Treasury, Transportation, and Energy; and, within the State Department, the Working Group on Terrorism (WGT). Carter's term in the White House, of course, ended with a massive "failure" in dealing with "terrorism": the Iran hostage crisis of 1979–80.

Not surprisingly, Ronald Reagan echoed Nixon in running a "law and order" campaign, this time with "terrorism" playing an even more prominent role. Exploiting public discontent with Carter's Iran policy, Reagan referred to the Iranians during the 1980 campaign as "barbarians" and "common criminals," and told a national television audience just days before the election that "terrorism" was a "scourge of civilization." The approach taken during the Reagan Administration appears to have been twofold. First, the types of structures created under Carter were expanded and given a higher public profile, making "counterterrorism" a central element of U.S. foreign policy. Second, covert action was massively expanded both abroad (in Nicaragua, for example) and at home, where the administration revived Nixon-era CIA and FBI domestic surveillance measures. In summary, one might say that under Reagan, "terrorism" became a sort of national preoccupation, facilitated by the public statements of top officials such as George Shultz and Jeane Kirkpatrick. That the U.S. population bought into the idea of "fighting terrorism" (and hence into the general definition of what was being fought) was indicated by the massive public support for the aforementioned 1986 bombing raid on Libya.

The government's steadily increasing preoccupation with "terrorism" had a direct impact on the research agendas of social scientists working in international relations, security studies, and other policy-related fields. By the mid-1970s, "terrorism" was fast becoming a cottage industry in academia; more than a dozen books were published on the subject in 1975 alone. Two years later "terrorism" received its intellectual baptism in the form of *Terrorism*, a journal edited by Yonah Alexander and published by the Institute for Studies in International Terrorism (ISIT) at SUNY-Oneonta. Walter Laqueur's *Terrorism Reader* appeared in 1978, positing a grand historical narrative of political violence beginning with tyrannicide in ancient Greece, progressing through Rome, medieval Europe, and nineteenth-century Russia, and culminating in the contemporary actions of groups such as the PFLP, the Irish Republican Army (IRA), and various Latin American revolutionary movements.

It is impossible to understand "terrorism" without understanding the close relationship between the government and the academy. When this relationship is expanded to include private think tanks, corporations, the media, and the military, we begin to see the full complexity of the institutional web in which "terrorism experts" have operated since the 1970s. An overview of contributors to *Terrorism* from its inception in 1977 through the first half of 1990 is useful in illustrating this complexity: a random selection includes a U.S. senator, a researcher at the Brookings Institution, the South African ambassador to the United States, a CBS news reporter, the Vice President of Chemical Bank, a military psychologist, and an anonymous contributor identified only as "an Italian who is in the forefront of control of terrorism in Italy." Institutional affiliations are all the more significant when we consider what we might call the "revolving door" factor: "terrorism experts" regularly pass between institutions, often working for more than one sequentially or even simultaneously. Thus Ray Cline, for example, worked at the highest levels of the CIA from 1949 to 1966, and later moved to Georgetown University. He was regularly interviewed by the news media, contributed two articles to *Terrorism*, and coauthored a 1984 book (*Terrorism: The Soviet Connection*) with Yonah Alexander. Alexander, in addition to his position at SUNY-Oneonta, worked as a liaison officer for Israel's Ministry of Trade and Industry. Brian Jenkins, one of the most visible "experts," did some of the earliest and most influential government-sponsored studies on "terrorism" in the 1970s while working at the Rand Corporation, a private research organization. He has gone on to work for Kroll Associates, a security consulting firm, to serve on the White House Commission on Aviation Safety and Security, and to appear regularly on the major U.S. television networks.

The ability of the same "experts" to appear in multiple institutions ensures not only that their personal views will be widely disseminated, but also that the range of available opinion on "terrorism" will be narrow, for virtually all those recognized as "experts" share a common set of assumptions. In fact, the dominant understanding of what constitutes "terrorism" has changed little in recent decades, even though a variety of individuals and groups have occupied the role of "terrorist." In the eyes of the "experts" who provided the initial framing of the issue in the 1970s, "terrorism" represented a fundamental challenge to the authority of the state. Under the dominant definition, however, "terrorism" could only be directed against particular kinds of states, namely, Western or pro-Western states such as the United States and other nations (such as England, West Germany, or Israel) that belonged to the anti-Soviet bloc. In other words, out of all the political violence in the world, the damning label of "terrorism" was applied only to violence that came from the Left or (less frequently and in the European context) from the far Right. Political violence carried out by or with the support of the United States and its allies, by contrast, was known by a host of less pejorative terms: counterinsurgency, counterterrorism, low-intensity conflict, self-defense, and war. As Noam Chomsky aptly puts it, "it is the other fellow's crimes, not our own comparable or worse ones" that constitute "terrorism."[2]

In a move that finds echoes in the current U.S. war, early "terrorism experts" spoke and wrote of an "international terrorist conspiracy" controlled by the KGB, thereby linking a new enemy ("terrorism") with an old one (communism). In addition, much of this early writing ominously invoked the specter of a "terrorist" movement populated by armies of disaffected young people, who were viewed as naively susceptible to the seductions of radicalism. "Today's terrorist comes from an affluent middle- or upper-class family that enjoys some social prestige," declared one 1977 study in the inaugural issue of the journal *Terrorism.* "The university served as the recruiting ground . . . and it was here that most terrorists were first exposed to the ideas of Marxism or other revolutionary theories."[3] This focus on young people ("rebelling sophomores," in the language of another study in the same journal)[4] fits perfectly within the power elite's larger preoccupation with the threat posed by young people—antiwar activists, Black Panthers, members of the New Left—within the United States.

In this sense, the 2001 "terrorism craze" seems, once again, to be eerily familiar: simply substitute "Muslims" for "youth," "jihad" or "fundamentalism" for "Marxism," and "breeding ground" (the racist phrase now being employed to describe the refugee camps, urban slums, and other poverty-stricken communities in the Middle East) for "recruiting ground." The ideologues of the "war on terrorism," heavily influenced by the misleading notion that there is a "clash of civilizations" between "Islam" and "the West" (see "Civilization versus Barbarism"), have turned to "terrorism" as a language within which to couch their defense of American power and privilege. They could not have done so, however, if their predecessors had not done such a successful job of defining "terrorism" in the first place.

## Making War on an Invention

What, then, is the lesson of this history? Is the invention of "terrorism" an example of what George Orwell had in mind when he wrote, in 1946, that "all issues are political issues, and politics itself is a mass of lies, evasions, folly, hatred, and schizophrenia"?[5] The short answer, of course, is yes, and in this sense the language of "terrorism" has much in common with the literally colorful language used in the past to designate the nation's enemies (the "Red Scare," the "Yellow Peril"), as well as with Orwell's own examples of political language ("pacification," "transfer of population"). Recognizing these connections, however, does not absolve us of the responsibility to analyze critically how the language of "terrorism" is being employed in 2001. This is no small task, for "terrorism" is closely linked with an entire vocabulary of equally questionable concepts, each of which has its own history. Moreover, as I have already suggested, the complexity of "terrorism" exists in stark contrast to the apparent simplicity and transparency that are implied by its usage in the phrase "war on terrorism." In the remainder of this essay I will limit myself to two main observations concerning this issue. First, the category of "terrorism" continues to be applied selectively, and in a way that serves the goals of U.S. policies, despite the fact that these very policies often cause or support more human suffering than is caused by the so-called "terrorists" the United States opposes. Ultimately this leads to operative official definitions of "terrorism" that are so vague and redundant as to defy logic, making it easier for the Bush Administration to generate public support for the war. Second, fueling the American obsession with "terrorism" diverts attention from a host of policies through which the United States has historically projected its imperial power, with disastrous results, in the Middle East.

As I have already suggested, "terrorism" is nothing more than a name given to a small subset of actions within the much larger category of political violence. What distinguishes "terrorism" from other acts of political violence, of course, depends on who is doing the defining (or nondefining, as we will see below). From the perspective of analysts who are concerned with defending U.S. economic and military supremacy, the safest definition, now as in the 1970s, is that "terrorism" involves organized opposition to the policies of the United States or its allies. By this definition, it is literally impossible for the U.S. government to commit or support acts of "terrorism." In this case, using the language of "terrorism"—and, at the extreme, declaring war on it— is one way for U.S. officials and supporters of U.S. policies to downplay the immense human suffering that continues to occur as a result of those policies.

Yet the evidence of this suffering is all around us, and this is where other existing definitions of "terrorism" run into the problem of double standards. Each possible definition has its referents in specific U.S. actions. Violence used to achieve political ends? The Vietnam War (or any other war). Violence perpetrated by nonstate actors against a sovereign state? The Nicaraguan *contras*. Violence committed by a nondemocratic government against its own population? The repression carried out by U.S.–trained dictators in Latin America. Violence targeting innocent civilians? The U.S. bombing of water-treatment facilities in Iraq during the Gulf War. Violence designed to create panic among a population and put pressure on their government? The bombing of Hiroshima and Nagasaki.

The point here is that *any* explicit definition of "terrorism" could be used to identify and condemn the actions of the United States and many of its allies. Maintaining the illusion of U.S. blamelessness, therefore, *requires that "terrorism" not be defined at all.* Consequently, instead of definitions we find tautological evasions. For example, when Secretary of State George Shultz gave a speech on "terrorism" to the Park Avenue Synagogue in New York in 1984, he offered a curious observation: "Terrorism is a modern barbarism that we call terrorism."[6] Seventeen years later, when George W. Bush addressed the U.S. Congress to declare his war on "terrorism," he could do no better, speaking vaguely of "terrorists" as "enemies of freedom." Any sense of the specificity of "terrorism"—that is, anything that might distinguish "terrorism" as a particular form of political violence—was lost when the president argued that the September 11 attacks were "an act of war" and that the perpetrators "follow in the path of fascism, Nazism and totalitarianism." A key statement by Secretary of Defense Donald Rumsfeld, published in the *New York Times* shortly before the United States began bombing Afghanistan, contained nothing resembling a definition; the war, Rumsfeld wrote, was simply against "terrorism's attack on our way of life."[7]

Perhaps the most telling moment in the current situation, however, occurred during the United Nations General Assembly's extraordinary weeklong (October 1–5, 2001) "Debate on measures to eliminate international terrorism."[8] Representatives of one hundred seventy nations rose to speak on the issue, and while all condemned the attacks of September 11, many also made careful reference to the double standards and blind spots inherent in the implicit, dominant definition of "terrorism." Moroccan ambassador Mohamed Bennouna pointedly argued that "security will not be universal until dire poverty suffered by increasing numbers of people is overcome as well as sheer humiliation and injustice worldwide to which are subject entire populations including children, either in Palestine or elsewhere." The Malaysian representative, Hasmy Agam, echoed a long-standing refrain of "Third World" leaders when he declared, "Malaysia condemns terrorism *in all its forms and manifestations*" (emphasis added), thereby drawing attention—subtly but unmistakably for anyone familiar with the debate—to the long history of Western imperialism. A proposed international conference, he said, "must examine the issue of terrorism comprehensively, including its definition." Such statements gain even greater force when we consider that they came on the heels of the UN–sponsored World Conference against Racism, when the U.S. delegation walked out rather than face questions about the devastation of slavery and the oppression of the Palestinians.

The remarks of many Western delegates during the General Assembly debate were equally telling. U.S. ambassador John Negroponte offered no definition of the topic under discussion, speaking instead of "barbarities," "chaos," and "the dark antithesis of the light we all want to see at the dawn of the new millennium." Representing the Netherlands, Dirk Jan van den Berg illustrated precisely the kind of tautology I have described. "[An] outstanding question in this context is the definition of terrorism. Much has been said on that score," he admitted, referring to the regular attempts of numerous nations to apply the label of "terrorism" to Israel, the United States, and others. "But 'ground zero' has made it painfully clear that terrorism in its true manifestation *defines itself.* There is no cause or grievance that can justify these kinds of acts. There is no distinction between good and bad terrorists. *There are just terrorists*" (emphasis added). His remarks followed those of UK representative Sir Peter Greenstock, who also offered token recognition of the Third World critiques, only to silence them with his own redundancy: "Increasingly, questions are being raised about the problem of the definition of a terrorist. Let us be wise and focused about this: *terrorism is terrorism*. . . . There is common ground amongst all of us on what constitutes terrorism. What looks, smells and kills like terrorism is terrorism" (emphasis added).

It should be noted that Greenstock is considerably less skilled in the art of nondefinition than many of his American and Israeli counterparts, for his remarks ironically give legitimacy to the perspectives of non-Western communities whose victimization has never been recognized in the dominant language of "terrorism." Palestinians, after all, know better than anyone that military occupation "looks, smells and kills like terrorism." Afghans, Iraqis, and Panamanians could say the same thing about aerial bombardment; Salvadorans and Guatemalans could testify to the "terrorism" of military death squads; Angolans, Cambodians, and Mozambicans are experts on the long-term terrorizing effects of land mines; Vietnamese and Lebanese have lived the horrible reality of chemical warfare in the form of napalm and phosphorous shells; and the list goes on. Taking the argument further, one could say that the global economy itself, organized and governed primarily according to the needs of U.S.–based transnational corporations, is the ultimate producer of "terror" for populations across the globe. What, after all, is more "terrifying" than systematic, widespread hunger and hopelessness? A Brazilian anarchist group perhaps had this point in mind when it circulated the following statement after the September 11 attacks:

> 35,615 children died out of starvation on September 11, 2001
> victims: 35,615 children (source: FAO)
> where: poor countries
> special tv programs: none
> newspaper articles: none
> messages from the president: none
> solidarity acts: none
> minutes of silence: none
> victims mournings: none

organized forums: none
pope messages: none
stock exchanges: didn't care
euro: kept its way
alert level: zero
army mobilization: none
conspiracy theories: none
main suspects: rich countries[9]

This is why tautology is safer than any sort of qualitative description. U.S. officials, having learned this lesson long ago, know that the best way to avoid the issue altogether is to locate "terrorism" squarely in the individuals upon whom public anger is periodically focused: Arafat, Khomeini, Saddam, bin Laden.

We are left, then, with a remarkable example of circular logic, with the political equivalent of a cat endlessly chasing its tail. The operative, unstated definition of "terrorism" at work in the "war on terrorism" runs roughly as follows: *"Terrorism" is what "terrorists" do. And who are the "terrorists"? Well, we know who they are, because we have already identified them—they are the ones who commit "terrorism."* Within such a closed circle, "terrorism" is congenital; it is a natural state of being for the "terrorist." Once again, it is important to note that this is not a new argument. The notion that "terrorism" can be fully explained with reference to pseudopsychology finds support in Benjamin Netanyahu's *Terrorism: How the West Can Win*, where the future prime minister tells his readers, "The root cause of terrorism lies not in grievances but in *a disposition toward unbridled violence.* . . . In this context, the observation that *the root cause of terrorism is terrorists* is more than a tautology" (emphasis added).[10] No matter how many times Bush Administration officials insist that they are not stigmatizing Arabs or Muslims, their use of the tautological definition of "terrorism" implicitly makes use of Netanyahu's racist logic; there is thus a direct link between the language of "terrorism" and the encouragement of racial and ethnic hatred.

As Edward Said and others have demonstrated, anti-Arab and anti-Muslim sentiment in the United States is also closely related to American policy in the Middle East. Three elements of that policy deserve mention here: unconditional U.S. support of Israel, even when Israel's government acts in direct violation of international law; United States backing of a host of repressive, undemocratic regimes throughout the Middle East; and regular U.S. military interventions in the region. The consistency with which the U.S. supports Israel in its repression of the Palestinians is exceeded only by the consistency of Israel's policy itself. In carrying out a range of violent measures—the illegal colonization of the West Bank and Gaza, the annexation of East Jerusalem, the invasion of Lebanon and siege of Beirut, the repression of the Palestinian *intifada*, and, most recently, the systematic use of political assassination—Israel has benefited from high levels of U.S. material aid and diplomatic protection, making the United States directly complicit in these actions. Meanwhile, in a breathtaking feat of public relations, Israeli leaders and policy scholars have managed to cultivate an image of themselves as the quintessential experts in "counterterrorism." (It is no accident that the thirty-year American obsession with "terrorism" coincides both with Israel's occupation of the West Bank and Gaza and with the consolidation of the U.S.–Israeli alliance.) Thus we find a guest on CNN reacting to September 11 by telling Americans that "we are all Israelis now." In such a view, there is no room for debate: Israel cannot commit "terrorism" any more than the United States can, for Israel's actions are never anything but a "response" to "terrorism."

The second pillar of U.S. policy in the Middle East is oil (see "Vital Interests"). The desire to secure access to oil, and to oppose popular Islamic movements, has led successive U.S. administrations to craft bilateral alliances and wartime "coalitions" not only with Israel, but also with Saudi Arabia, Egypt, Pakistan, Jordan, and a range of other countries where the commitment to democracy and human rights is in short supply. When U.S. ambassador Negroponte told the UN General Assembly in October 2001 that the United States "helped defend Muslims in Kuwait," he glossed over the fact that the United States has always placed oil over humanity in its Middle East policy, happily propping up autocratic leaders (including the Kuwaiti royal family) as long as they keep the pipeline open. "Far better to have a Mubarak or a King Abdullah or a King Fahd running the show," writes journalist Robert Fisk sarcastically, "than to let the Arabs vote for a real government that might oppose US policies in the region."[11] In this respect, the current U.S. "petropolicy" has much in common with the destructive U.S. role in Central America during the Reagan years: instead of "containing" socialism at the expense of democracy, we are now containing Islamic populism at the expense of democracy.

The "war on terrorism," of course, illustrates yet again that unjust policies inevitably require the periodic use of force to keep in place the conditions that enable those policies to run smoothly. Direct U.S. military intervention in the Middle East dates back to 1958, when U.S. Marines went to Lebanon to preserve "stability" in that country; by that time, the CIA had already been active in the region, helping to overthrow a democratically elected regime in Iran in 1953 after the regime moved to nationalize its oil supply (see "Freedom" and "Blowback"). Later interventions include sending U.S. Marines to Lebanon once again in 1983 to support one side in the civil war there; the 1991 Gulf War and subsequent sanctions against Iraq, which killed hundreds of thousands of civilians but left Saddam Hussein in power; the 1998 destruction of a pharmaceutical plant in Sudan on the mistaken assumption that it was a chemical weapons facility linked with Osama bin Laden; and the provision of military aid, hardware, and training to Israel, Iran, Iraq, Turkey, Saudi Arabia, and the *mujáhiddín* fighting the Soviet occupation of Afghanistan.

Such policies do not serve the cause of democracy in the Middle East; on the contrary, as Turkish novelist Orhan Pamuk writes in a recent commentary, they simply ensure a continuing cycle of violence. "What prompts an impoverished old man in Istanbul to condone the terror in New York in a moment of anger, or a Palestinian youth fed up with Israeli oppression to admire the Taliban, who throw nitric acid at women because they reveal their faces?" Pamuk asks. "It is the feeling of impotence deriving from degradation, the failure to be understood, and the inability of such people to make their voices heard."[12]

Given the nature of U.S. policy in the Middle East, what are Americans to think about Arabs and Muslims? U.S. support for Israel suggests that Arabs are irrationally bent on opposing, even destroying Israel; U.S. backing of repressive regimes suggests that Arabs and Muslims are incapable or undeserving of the same democratic rights the United States claims to champion; and U.S. "petropolicy" implies that Arabs exist primarily for the purpose of providing us with access to cheap fossil fuels for our plastics, our sport-utility vehicles, and our military arsenal. In this light, is it any wonder that racism against Arabs—including the identification of the Arabs and Islam with "terrorism"—continues to run rampant and unchecked in the United States while American flags fly and the bombs rain down on Afghanistan?

**NOTES**

1. Edward Said, "The Essential Terrorist," in Edward Said and Christopher Hitchens (eds.), *Blaming the Victims: Spurious Scholarship and the Palestinian Question* (London: Verso, 1988), 158.

2. Noam Chomsky, "Terrorism and American Ideology," in Edward Said

and Christopher Hitchens (eds.), *Blaming the Victims: Spurious Scholarship and the Palestinian Question* (London: Verso, 1988), 119.

3. Charles A. Russell and Bowman H. Miller, "Profile of a Terrorist," *Terrorism: An International Journal* 1, 1 (1977): 17.

4. Conrad V. Hassel, "Terror: The Crime of the Privileged," *Terrorism: An International Journal* 1, 1 (1977): 4.

5. George Orwell, "Politics and the English Language," in *The Orwell Reader* (New York: Harcourt, Brace and Company, 1956), 363–64.

6. Eqbal Ahmad, "Terrorism: Theirs and Ours," lecture given at the University of Colorado at Boulder, October 12, 1998 (http://www.sangam.org/ANALYSIS/Ahmad.htm).

7. Donald Rumsfeld, "A New Kind of War," *New York Times*, September 27, 2001.

8. All transcripts of the General Assembly debate were accessed in October 2001 at http://www.un.org/terrorism/list011005.html.

9. Forwarded e-mail from Agencia de Noticias Anarquistas (Brazil), September 20, 2001.

10. Robert Fisk, "Farewell to Democracy in Pakistan," *Independent* (London), October 26, 2001 (http://www.independent.co.uk/story.jsp?story=101459).

11. Quoted in Said, "The Essential Terrorist," 154.

12. Orhan Pamuk, "The Anger of the Damned," *New York Review of Books*, November 15, 2001.

## SUGGESTIONS FOR FURTHER READING

Ahmad, Eqbal. *Terrorism: Theirs and Ours* (Open Media Pamphlet Series). New York: Seven Stories Press, 2001.

Chomsky, Noam. "Terrorism and American Ideology." In *Blaming the Victims: Spurious Scholarship and the Palestinian Question*, ed. Edward Said and Christopher Hitchens. London: Verso, 1988.

Herman, Edward S. *The Real Terror Network: Terrorism in Fact and Propaganda.* Boston: South End Press, 1998.

Herman, Edward S., and Gerry O'Sullivan. *The Terrorism Industry: The Experts and Institutions That Shape Our View of Terror.* New York: Pantheon Books, 1989.

*Middle East Report.* Published four times annually by the Middle East Research and Information Project (MERIP), Washington, D.C.

Said, Edward. "The Essential Terrorist." In *Blaming the Victims: Spurious Scholarship and the Palestinian Question*, ed. Edward Said and Christopher Hitchens. London: Verso, 1988.

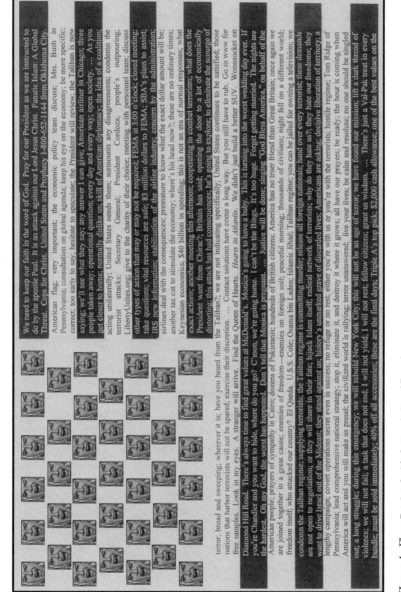

Zone 4, *Flag*. Reprinted with the permission of *Zone 4*.

# 12. Unity

EVE WALSH STODDARD AND
GRANT H. CORNWELL

## Unity as Moral Imperative

The events of September 11 have brought the ethics of unity into
the foreground of public discourse. How can a call for unity be a
bad thing? Whereas the term "nation" used to be understood as
a population of people bound together by common descent, language, culture, or history, most scholars now see nations as
largely "imagined communities" where the elements of identity,
the things that bind a group together, are features of stories the
group tells itself about itself. In the current moment the "American" nation is being defined by the events of September 11. This
is what "we" have in common. "Unity" means sharing this moment. It means standing together with other Americans, but it
also means standing against those responsible for the events. In
this essay we will suggest what is dangerous about the current call
for unity, that it contradicts essential principles of "America" that
we are being called upon to rally around.

In the current climate, nuanced differences of all sorts have
been distilled into the moral logic of unity. Diversity of identity
and opinion have been reduced by both government and the
media to a binary logic expressed in President Bush's stark dual-
ism, "you are for us or against us." In the context of the era of
American multiculturalism, where the moral emphasis in "*E
Pluribus Unum*" has been on pluralism, September 11 violently

shifted the emphasis to the other term. The diversity that American popular culture has learned to recognize, if not celebrate, is now eclipsed by the mandate for unity. Within the United States unity has become a moral imperative, with the U.S. flag as its icon and "United we stand" its motto.

While one might be tempted to equate these signifiers of oneness with old-fashioned American patriotism, in fact they have a born-again, globalized twist that represents a break with past slogans and Fourth of July picnics. The complex processes of globalization have created important linkages across state boundaries and inside them. The discourse of the so-called "War on Terror" vividly illustrates this. In the days following September 11, politicians and journalists around the world adopted the rhetoric of "We are all Americans." The United States and Britain bombed Afghanistan in an effort to "root out" the leadership of a loosely networked, dispersed set of allies trying to undermine U.S. intervention in the Middle East. The people construed as the enemy, al-Qaeda, are by and large not Afghan nationals, but rather Saudi Arabian. The state of Saudi Arabia is an ally of the United States. Thus key entities in what was inter*national* relations have become despatialized and disjoined from nation-state containers. Bombs have to be aimed at spatial locations, and they are not normally aimed at friendly states, even when there are criminals within those states. The normal mode of dealing with small groups of terrorists or criminals is some form of criminal justice process such as the trials of those accused in the Lockerbie bombing of Pan Am flight 103 or those accused of bombing the U.S. embassies in East Africa. In "the War on Terror," the enemy is both within and without the United States.

Similarly, the discourse of unity applies to social entities both smaller and larger than the entity of the United States of America. It applies to New York City, whose global status as a financial center, and now as a victim of a major bombing, transcends its role as simply a major U.S. city. New York City has long been characterized as a locus of migration and cultural heterogeneity, hence Ellis Island and the Statue of Liberty. New York's iconic status as a port of entry to immigrants is known around the world, not just within the United States. But as of September 11, New York has become a signifier of the highest and most generous forms of human solidarity, and money has poured in from around the United States and beyond its borders to aid the families of those who were killed at the World Trade Center. Interestingly, the global emotional response, as portrayed in the media, and as experienced by Americans abroad, enacted an identification with the wounding of New York, of the United States, and of global capitalism, that goes far beyond the kind of international response normally given to disasters, whether humanly or naturally caused. To give one example of the discourse:

> Now, we are all New Yorkers. And we are all proud of the New Yorkers and Washingtonians who rushed to respond to the crime against America and humanity. In a sense, too, the whole world was American on Tuesday, sharing in the suffering inflicted by vicious mass-murderers. Make no mistake, humanity regards this as a crime against all peoples. Around the world, people with any hold on moral values are appalled at the barbarism of the crimes' perpetrators. In Beijing, horrified people watched their TVs into the middle of the night. From Perth, Australia, a 15-year-old girl named Sarah e-mailed this newspaper enclosing a poem she had written and a note that ended: "Thank you for all you have done, America, and even though I am not American I cry in sorrow . . . GOD SAVE AMERICA!"[1]

It is possible that the superpower, when victimized and wounded, becomes a more humanized and identifiable entity or that less powerful nations who might resent the United States under normal circumstances have become used to relying on its might as a hedge against more directly threatening enemies. It is also possible that the export of American media, whether Hollywood films, TV shows, or broadcast news has so saturated the world with images of New York that a global audience truly can perceive the chief icons of the city, like the World Trade Center or the Statue of Liberty, as objects of sentimental attachment. To identify with New York is to identify with a global city, not a nation-state with a major military presence in the world. To identify with New Yorkers after September 11 was to empathize with the horror that struck thousands dead in the midst of an ordinary working day. But that "We are all New Yorkers now" slid very quickly on the part of many speakers into the quite different, "We are all Americans now."

On the international front, such recent enemies as Iran and Russia have given support to the U.S. war efforts, and European allies like France who have been critical of U.S. military strikes in the past two decades have given total support, because "We are all Americans now." As Daryl Lindsey and Steve Kettmann write,

> it all represents a dizzying turnaround from the turbulence in U.S.-European relations that had generated so much press attention in the first months of the Bush administration. . . . The split over global-warming policy culminated in July with the European agreement in Bonn, Germany to go ahead with the Kyoto process, even without the U.S. This week, that was all forgotten—at least for the time being—along with European worries about Bush's mania for missile defense. Like Tony Blair, Schroeder could hardly have been a more steadfast, even passionate, ally in the wake of the attacks Tuesday. Visibly shaken, Schroeder told the German parliament Wednesday that the terrorist attack was "a declaration of war against the entire civilized world," earning a unanimous show of applause from different political parties. . . . As Peter Struck, a Social Democrat parliamentary leader, said simply: "Today we are all Americans."[2]

This rhetorical identification with the United States, having spread across the globe at the speed of e-mail, makes the meaning of unity after September 11 different from that of traditional patriotism, though it is signified by the same icons and symbols. All intranational and even to a large degree *inter*national differences have been submerged and erased under the sign of the flag, the U.S. stars and stripes, the icon of unity. Thus Queen Elizabeth, for the first time in her almost fifty-year reign, altered the ceremonial Changing of the Guard at Buckingham Palace to incorporate the U.S. national anthem.

As time has passed since September 11, the media focus has shifted from "Ground Zero," the immense rubble in Lower Manhattan, to "America's New War." CNN constructed daily life in the aftermath of the attacks as a drama with unfolding acts. We know which act we are in by the emblazoned headline on top of the screen, from "America under Attack," to "America Strikes Back," to "America's New War," to "America Recovers." The actual news stories run at the bottom of the screen in small print while there are pictures or newscasters talking in the middle half of the screen. This new format downplays the importance of actual news stories, and replaces reporting with melodrama.

## The Flag as Icon

Throughout American society, the call for unity is being heralded with images and icons. Words are not needed; one need only attach a flag to one's house or car or backpack. According to CNN, Walmart sold 450,000 American flags between Tuesday September 11 and Thursday September 13, compared to 26,000 for the same period the year before. Kmart sold 200,000 in the same period. Many stores across the United States ran out of flags quickly. Kmart's website's top seller was a T-shirt with the flag and the motto "United We Stand."³ There is a website for something called "The Unity Ribbon," a ribbon with red and white stripes and white stars on a blue field. The ribbon can be imported into other websites and hundreds of businesses and individuals are listed as having adopted it. The creators of the unity ribbon wanted to find a way to "help draw people back together, help them *unite!*" They realized there was no "better symbol of American pride and unity than the American Flag." The image of the unity ribbon can be seen on magazines and local newspapers, on people's screen savers, everywhere.

What does the flag mean? The White House website has a special section produced in the wake of September 11, called "Standing for the Flag." President Bush introduces the pictures of the flag as follows: "Now, as the country stares down a new peril, Americans are flying the banner proudly, heeding its call for unity. . . . America protects the freedom our flag represents by displaying it in many ways, at our homes, as ribbons and pins, in our actions and as photographs as is displayed here." The presence of the flag on houses, cars, clothing, and magazines is a powerful sign of apparent unity. Yet that sign of unity is possible in part because the flag is just an icon, not words, and as such it carries many meanings. For example, many people see the flag as a sign of sympathy and support for those who died in the September 11 attacks. One college student said that, having lost friends in the World Trade Center, when she sees flags she feels cheered up by the emotional solidarity they offer. But many others see the flag as a sign of support specifically for the military personnel engaged in attacks on Afghanistan. Others display the flag as an expression of American defiance, support for war as retributive justice (see "Justice"). Yet others take comfort in the traditions of American nationhood associated with the flag and fly it as an expression of faith that the nation will endure.

What is interesting is that all those displaying the flag have a sense of solidarity with others who display it, even if the specific motives vary greatly. Nonetheless when people *do* start discussing the meaning of the flag, emotions flare. Unity takes precedence over freedom in such debates. The passions currently associated with the flag allow little room for the dissent that is a hallmark of democracy. As one student said in a recent forum, "I get so angry at some people's attitudes about the flag that I want to use fists instead of words." Thus unity around the flag is ambiguously both willing and enforced.

Yet there is ample evidence that not all U.S. citizens share this feeling of unity. Jemimah Noonoo, a university student of color, wrote an article in her student newspaper on the feelings of African Americans about the current situation. She quotes columnist Mary Mitchell of the *Chicago Sun-Times* on her decision to put a flag in her car and in her house: "'she never flew the flag before," Mitchell wrote, "Frankly, patriotism hasn't been part of my experience. That is the impact racism has had on countless black Americans. It is impossible for people to live through periods of slavery, lynching, segregation, unfair treatment and bigotry and emerge bursting with national pride.'" Noonoo writes,

> Viewed as the negative "other," "inferior" and "culturally de-
> prived" by the dominant culture, most black Americans often
> have wondered if true citizenship rights are only extended to
> whites. . . . Though media portraits of blacks and whites pray-
> ing together, crying together and healing together are power-
> ful images, these snapshots purport the dangerous myth that,
> by virtue of terrorist attack, America has confronted and truly
> overcome its ugly past.[4]

In a class at another university, there were sharp differences in attitude between students of color and white students about flying the American flag. African American students stated emphatically that the flag represented a nation that had done nothing but oppress their people and they could not imagine identifying with it. "This war is between them and them," said one. "I have disappeared as an American. This isn't about me, and my people and my issues have been erased. Where I live in the city, we live in another world. We aren't from the America that is at war." These sentiments suggest that there are unseen parameters of race and class that mark the boundaries of unity. One would expect that an open discussion of who is included and who is excluded in the sentiment of unity would be a vibrant element of American civic discourse. That this discussion is not happening is a cause for concern.

## Unity as Coercion, Global and Local

From her perspective in South Asia, the Indian novelist Arundhati Roy writes that "Governments . . . use flags first to shrink-wrap people's minds and smother thought, and then as ceremonial shrouds to bury their willing dead." Thus, beyond the immediate emotional and sympathetic response of identity with U.S. wounds, there have emerged in the months since September 11, new, coercive forms of unity both within the United States and around the world. In these more coercive forms of solidarity the major contradiction that haunts U.S. ideology reveals itself. The discourse surrounding the flag identifies it as symbolizing both *unity* and *freedom*. But freedom in a democratic context always includes a dimension of dissent. In this sense, the current discipline of unity is undemocratic and therefore un-American. In its own creation narrative, "America" is a nation born out of dissent; resistance, critique, and opposition are the nation's founding motives. They form the nation's political epistemology: the idea that political wisdom emerges from a process of open contest where opposing views are weighed against one another, held in this way to high standards of evidence and reasoning. Vig-

orous public debate over policy and meaning is thought to safeguard against a society where the analysis or opinion of an elite
stands as public truth.

Unity, then, is something to be suspicious of, to worry about.
Where there is unity there is no opposition, and where there is
no opposition there is no democracy. Within U.S. society, an impression has been created through flag displays and television
talk shows that there is no space for freedom of thought or expression about the "new war." One is made to feel alone, isolated
in opposition. The mainstream media creates the feeling that it
is unpatriotic to criticize the univocal voice of patriarchal authority. For instance, in numerous interviews and talk shows, one
hears commentary about the limitations on stand-up comedians
for whom presidents and government actions are major fodder.
The consensus now is that it would be wrong, if not treasonous,
to make fun of G. W. Bush, so recently the butt of many jokes
about anti-intellectualism and ignorance of foreign affairs. Immediately following September 11, lists of inappropriate songs
circulated around radio stations. These included John Lennon's
utopian "Imagine," which blames religions for many of the
world's wars and persecutions. In a speech on September 30, Al
Gore, in a call for unity, declared, "George W. Bush is my com-
mander in chief." These are the real un-American moments.
They are a kind of compulsory unity that is at odds with the
American mythos.

This compulsory unity became official in the congressional
vote giving Bush broad authority to use military force against
"terror." Out of 535 members of Congress, only *one* person voted
no, Representative Barbara Lee (D-Oakland). In an *L.A. Times*
interview, Marc Cooper asked her, "In the days following the
vote, you were discussed widely on talk radio. People called you
a traitor. They called you un-American and an accomplice of the
terrorists. How do you respond to charges like that?" Lee's response is instructive, and it is a frightening reminder about what

it is that unity erases. "I am an American who has tried to protect our democracy, who has tried to protect our system of checks and balances," she said. "If I hadn't, in the moment of adversity, tried to make sure that our Constitution stayed in place, that would have been an abdication of my responsibility as an American citizen and as a representative."[5] Yet for voting her conscience and trying to represent the people of Oakland, Lee was reviled as a sympathizer with those who flew into the World Trade Center.

As time has passed since the immediate shock of the September 11 attacks, it has been somewhat easier to voice doubts about U.S. policy both as the partial cause of the attacks and in response to them, but as of early November, Bush's approval ratings were still at nearly 90 percent. There are alternative and oppositional voices in the media, but one has to seek them out. According to *Newsweek's* cover story on the 9-11 Generation, even on college campuses about 85 percent of the students are united in support of Bush and the war. Nonetheless it is important to remember that 15 percent of the population opposed to the war is significant and is likely to grow into a larger movement as time passes and more word of "collateral damage" reaches audiences in the West. The protests over the Vietnam War began with a small radical group and eventually spread to a much more moderate, large group of students.

Perhaps most corrosive of what the U.S. flag is supposed to represent, "liberty and justice for all," is the virtually total assent of the mainstream news media to the project of unity. The role of the press in a democracy is to be a watchdog, to stand apart from the government and present multiple perspectives on its actions and policies. Yet since September 11, newscasters have openly wept and praised the president. They have implied that dissidents are sympathizers with the terrorists. On November 4, CNN's Larry King had as guests Walter Cronkite, longtime CBS anchor, and Dan Rather, his replacement. These are representatives of competing news networks, yet Rather exuded patriotic fervor as he joined with King in praising the president. It was noticeable that Cronkite, a newscaster of a former era, did not participate in the judgments of the government, but restricted his comments to expressing a desire to be on the scene as a reporter.

On the global level, the coercive pressure for unity is overt and backed up by threats of force. On September 20, in his joint address to Congress, the president set up the situation as follows: "On September 11th, enemies of freedom committed an act of war against our country," claiming that the target was democracy and freedoms, of religion, speech, voting, assembling, and disagreeing with each other. Bush stated, "Every nation, in every region, now has a decision to make. Either you are with us, or you are with the terrorists. This is the world's fight. This is civilization's fight. . . . The civilized world is rallying to America's side." This kind of language is a thinly veiled threat to Muslim states because there has been much talk about bombing other nations in addition to Afghanistan. He also said, "the name of today's military operation is Enduring Freedom. We defend not only our precious freedoms, but also the freedom of people everywhere to live and raise their children free from fear." Thus the discourse of freedom is invoked to legitimate the destruction of various groups' civil liberties at home in the United States (immigrants held under suspicion with no charges and no hearing), in countries pressured into supporting U.S. military actions in Afghanistan, and in Afghanistan itself, where civilians are being killed by U.S. bombs (see "Freedom").

## Unity and Diversity: The Erasure of Inequalities

The motto of the United States is *E Pluribus Unum*: "Out of many, one." While the "many" in the motto may refer specifically to states comprising the Union, it expresses a tension that runs across different discourses, at different points in time, since the inception of the nation. The many have been the libertarian individuals demanding the right to bear arms, they have been the Confederate States in the Civil War, they have been communist sympathizers during the McCarthy era, they have been the antiwar protestors in the Vietnam era, they have been women seeking the vote, and they have been African Americans and Native Americans excluded from the founding vision of the United States. Nonetheless, the discursive tradition of Enlightenment rights that empowered the Founding Fathers has also provided leverage for dissent and demonstration, the tradition of civil disobedience inscribed by Thoreau, the civil rights movement, and other forms of resistance and opposition.

The culture wars of the past two decades pitted the discourse of the many, of multiculturalism and diversity, against the rhetoric of unity. The conservatives argued that patriotism and nationhood were being destroyed by a recognition of diversity. Nonetheless, the side of the debate championing diversity had gained a great deal of public credence by the end of the century. This was shown in the demand of elite white students for diverse college experiences and the representations of diverse workplaces in Fortune 500 TV commercials.

One of the wrecks left by the September 11 attacks and subsequent "War on Terror" is any domestic agenda for dealing with inequality. Just before the attacks, and perhaps not coincidentally, the United States failed to send a high-level delegation to the UN conference on racism at Durban, South Africa. Thus one of the questions arising from the pressure for unity right now is where does racial and ethnic diversity fit in? President Bush has clearly called for a cessation of domestic violence against American Muslims and persons of South Asian appearance, but there have been many instances of such violence, even murder. The lack of knowledge of most Americans about the Islamic world and Central and South Asia has been evident in the targeting of such groups as Sikhs, who bear no relation to al-Qaeda, the Arab world, or Afghanistan, but happen to wear turbans. Also just prior to the attacks, the U.S. Border Patrol was under criticism for racial profiling, as were metropolitan police in several areas of the United States. The groups most often profiled were African Americans, and on the southern border, people of Mexican or Central American appearance. In the aftermath of the attacks, there was a spate of commentary and editorials on radio and television featuring African Americans confessing that they were now themselves participating in racial profiling, as they scrutinized Middle Eastern or South Asian looking people on planes. This is meant to legitimate not only racial profiling but xenophobia. The editorial page of the *New York Times* for October 12 includes a letter from Wendy Eisner claiming that many black people have gained a stronger sense of themselves as Americans since the attacks and that this affirmation shows the world that the United States is a "shining example of unity amid diversity."

Niels Kjellerup, Editor and Senior Partner of Resource International in Australia and editor of a web-based forum for managers of call centers, published on his website an opinion piece on September 11 also published in *Le Monde*. In the essay Kjellerup brings together antiterrorism and suppression of civil liberties at home. He says, "Political correctness ended on this day in the realization that Evil must be confronted and called by its real name. Terrorists are not misguided youth, but fanatical killers. I no longer want to understand the motivation of Terrorists & the social diseases which allow such sentiments to grow, as an excuse for not acting to prevent their deeds."[6] "Political correctness" is a catch-all term invented by the Right to characterize efforts toward social justice and equality for people of color, gays and lesbians, women, the handicapped, and other marginalized groups. His response implies that he is among those conservatives who have merely tolerated efforts to liberate the marginalized members of Western societies from inequality and oppression. The articles on call center management that he has published on the web show that he is very much in favor of trade liberalization and economic globalization as these policies have made possible the "outsourcing" of telemarketing from the United States to remote locations in the world. Thus one might infer that people like him, while they deplore the violence committed on September 11, find a silver lining in the cloud of the World Trade Center. The antiterrorism movement is sweeping away leftist efforts to address inequality. Kjellerup is prophetic in acclaiming a unity which will mute the recognition of domestic diversities.

The mainstream media gives the impression that all Americans, of every color, are part of the unity agenda. Many may be, but then again, it is a difficult climate in which to express dissent. Whenever someone on a news talk show tried to talk about the reasons why many people in the world resent the United States, the commentators would immediately accuse them of supporting the terrorist attacks. It has become de rigueur to preface any kind of qualified approval or dissent by repeating over and over that one condemns the acts of September 11. There is little discursive space for feeling terrible about the attacks but at the same time arguing against retaliation and for U.S. policy changes in the Middle East.

The attack on the World Trade Center has unleashed a repressed desire for patriotic innocence, for a common enemy, for a Star Wars narrative of good and evil. National Public Radio has been rife with comments by listeners who express the joy of finding unity, from the senior citizen who hearkens back nostalgically to an allegedly pure patriotism during World War II, to the Generation X member who exults in discovering a consciousness beyond cynicism, a first experience with believing in something positive about her country. The lessons of Vietnam lurk between

World War II and September 11, 2001, and society wants them to be a hurdle overcome, a nightmare we have awoken from rather than a warning about historical amnesia.

## NOTES

1. "We Are All New Yorkers," *Daily Herald* (Everett, Wash.), September 13, 2001 (http://www.heraldnet.com/Stories/01/9/13/).
2. Daryl Lindsey and Steve Kettmann, "We Are All Americans," September 13, 2001 (http://www.salon.com/news/feature/2001/09/13/germany/index.html).
3. "Sales Spike for Red, White and Blue," CNN.com September 14, 2001 (http://www.cnn.com/2001/US/09/14/flag.sales/).
4. Jemimah Noonoo, "We're All Americans—For Now," *Chicago Flame*, October 2, 2001 (http://www.chicagoflame.com/issues_2001/100201/opinions_oped4.html).
5. Marc Cooper, "Rep. Barbara Lee: Rowing against the Tide," *Los Angeles Times*, September 23, 2001 (http://www.latimes.com/news/nation-world/nation/la-092301intv.story).
6. Niels Kjellerup, "We're ALL Americans," Call Center Managers Forum (http://www.callcentres.com.au/).

## SUGGESTIONS FOR FURTHER READING

Boime, Albert. *The Unveiling of the National Icons: A Plea for Patriotic Iconoclasm in a Nationalist Era*. Cambridge: Cambridge University Press, 1998.

Glenn, David. "The War on Campus." *Nation*, December 3, 2001 (http://thenation.com).

Martin, Jerry L., and Anne D. Neal. "Defending Civilization: How Our Universities Are Failing America and What Can Be Done about It." Washington, D.C.: American Council of Trustees and Administrators, 2001 (http://www.goacta.org).

Mill, John Stuart. *On Liberty*. Indianapolis: Bobbs-Merrill, 1956.

Nussbaum, Martha C., and Respondents. *For Love of Country: Debating the Limits of Patriotism*. Boston: Beacon Books, 1996.

Thoreau, Henry David. "Civil Disobedience." In *Walden*. New York: Signet Classic, 1980.

Ross Glover, *Crude Binary*. Reprinted with the permission of Ross Glover.

# 13. Vital Interests

## A Memoirist's Crash (Site) Course in U.S. Oil Consumption

NATALIA RACHEL SINGER

*Any time a new SUV rolls out of a U.S. car dealership, the leaders of those countries which are often referred to as "state sponsors of terrorism" must be laughing all the way to the bank. After all, global terrorism is partially funded through the sale of essentially one commodity: oil.*
*—theGlobalist,* October 17, 2001

I smelled the smoking rubble of the World Trade Center before we got close to it, before my friend Cathy and I had walked halfway through Soho. I knew that this mass grave would secrete its own horrific odors, but it was the acrid, chemical stench of sheetrock, metals, and rubber lit by petroleum products that I blamed for my headache and nausea and raw throat, and for both a déjà vu and dread I have yet to recover from. New Yorkers had been complaining about the fumes in the month since the attack, and my stepson, an art student at Cooper Union, had told me about needing a mask when the wind went uptown, but I suppose nothing really prepares you for an assault on the senses and the heart.

If smells take you to memory, to the madeleines of childhood, I was transported to industrial Ohio, a time and place of big factories, big cars, oil slicks on stinky chemical rivers, and an economy greased by big pre-Oil Embargo, pre-Earth Day dreams. As we walked further south, I found myself heading closer to the burning rubber of Akron and its Goodyear Tire factory, where the car I was in with some older teens broke down; and to the humid air of my neighborhood in Cleveland, which reeked of sulfur dioxide and gasoline; and to the smokestacks of Acorn Chemical Corporation in downtown Cleveland, where my grandmother kept the books to get away from her abusive husband. I grew up believing that sunsets were supposed to be a hazy orange-magenta, and such a faulty grasp of basic science was not helped by what happened in 1969, when it turned out that fire and water were not antagonists after all. When the Cuyahoga caught fire, I, a too-sensitive eleven-year-old in a self-combusting family in a rioting, burned-out city, was saddened but hardly surprised.

What ignited the World Trade Center towers, we all know now, was rage, along with the explosive power of two full tanks of airline fuel. Both the politics and the science of this were difficult and terrible for me to comprehend but I felt compelled to try, which is why I was headed toward the still-burning site of devastation. I hadn't lost any loved ones in the attack, but it felt as though I had. Cathy felt the same way.

If Cathy and I were the type of people to wear apparel advertising our likes and dislikes, we would each have heaps of "I Love New York" T-shirts. Cathy started taking the train from Poughkeepsie into Manhattan in ninth grade, when her mother bought her tickets to Broadway matinees and encouraged her, an aspiring artist, to check out the galleries of Soho. I started coming after college, twenty-two years ago, when Cindy and Dawn, friends from my Midwestern dorm, got magazine jobs in Manhattan, met their husbands, and settled down. Whether I was in town for work or to see my friends and, in recent years, my stepson, I always caught a show and an art exhibit and, like many visitors, fantasized a parallel life for myself in this roiling, pulsing maw of America's cultural capital.

Although Cathy and I work at a university seven hours to the north, what happens in New York City is always, for both of us, of vital interest.

But now, as we headed further south on Broadway past Tribeca, I began to wonder why I'd been so determined to make this trek. Our husbands had said in so many words that we were sick voyeurs. Maybe we were. I did, indeed, feel increasingly like an interloper in a zone of suffering, the stranger who crashes the funeral. On our walk we had already seen photos of lost loved ones claiming nearly every tree and billboard and kiosk. They were often of celebrations: graduations, birthdays, weddings. Every fire station was now a shrine covered with photographs, flowers, children's drawings, and banner tributes from schools as far away as Utah. Sometimes we'd also seen signs either advocating or protesting the five-day-old war—a war that made me feel hopeless about the millions of Afghans who would starve and the hundreds of suicide bombers who would be born in each village of civilians demolished by our cluster bombs. Between the evidence of all this death and the prospect of so much more, I found myself retreating to the kind of helpless passivity I'd known in childhood when my family lit up cigarettes and argued, flailing fists, and the TV blared images of boys in body bags and jungle villages on fire.

I was glad Cathy was navigating. I felt lost, dislocated in space and time, which was complicated by the fact that in all my years of coming to the city, I'd never been to the Financial District, not even when I was visiting Cindy, whose husband, Harry, worked at the World Trade Center, in the South Tower, as a vice president at Morgan Stanley. On September 11, Cindy had e-mailed me to say that Harry had evacuated his staff on the sixty-seventh floor even as a security guy on the forty-fourth floor, where it was necessary to change stairwells, was urging everyone to stay inside. Harry even half-dragged a heavy asthmatic woman down those sixty-seven flights of stairs, and his courage was such that a feature on him was picked up on the AP wire, and then, the ABC World News. I regretted that I'd never gone with her to have lunch with him at Windows on the World.

At the intersection of West Broadway and Duane, we stopped so Cathy could take a picture of the blocks and blocks of trucks lined up to haul away debris. I covered my nostrils with the tail of my denim shirt, wondering what chemical chain reactions were taking place in my nose as the diesel fumes spiked the particulate matter of combusted steel, cement, and rubber.

I felt that I should take notes, but I couldn't. Instead, I let certain images burn themselves into my brain: a female cop riding a golf cart; two slouching army reserves men looking bored, the soot piled in crevices of mock Corinthian columns and ledges of buildings; the vendors hawking American flags and photos of the World Trade Center towers intact. Cathy felt shy about taking pictures, but when we got to the first barricade, at Broadway and Fulton, we saw that a silent crowd of about fifty people were taking photographs too. A man flashed some ID to a policeman and was allowed to pass the gate with his small son and a grocery cart to head for home, presumably to an apartment where they might have witnessed the attack, where their furniture, curtains, and hair would remain acrid with the fumes for who-knows-how-long. It alarmed me that neither of them was wearing a mask.

I had checked the EPA web page before we left, and the New York page said the air was fine—no asbestos to worry over, all's well—but I wondered why they were only checking for asbestos. As I searched the crowds for signs of people protecting themselves with masks—few were—I found myself picturing the hundreds of oil fields set ablaze in the Gulf War both by our bombs and by retreating Iraqi troops, and I remembered the U.S. Defense Department's denials that the fumes of burning petroleum products were harmful to human health. At the moment, this thought seemed disconnected to the issue at hand, which I chalked up to my physical malaise: I wasn't even near the rubble of Ground Zero and the chemical air was making me headachy, queasy, dizzy, and disoriented. What was going to happen to all the rescue workers and police and fire fighters who had been working at the site twelve hours a day or more since the attacks? What was this stuff we were inhaling? Why hadn't I studied harder in tenth-grade chemistry?

(In fact, less than two weeks after we got back, I'd find out that I'd been right to worry: EPA data now revealed that the air near the site was full of benzene fumes, sulfur dioxide, copper, aluminum, and lead, while runoff into the Hudson was awash with PCBs, chromium, and chlorine dioxins. The health problems those working near the site could encounter—leukemia, kidney and lung disease, among others—may not appear for years.)

We headed west, toward Church Street. I still couldn't speak. I watched as Cathy photographed the smoky debris-smudged signs for a florist shop, a jeweler's, a beauty salon's, and a Cajun grill with the bannered plea to "Please try a free sample of flame broiled" chicken. The irony of this offer, coupled with the determination of the local businessmen to stay afloat amidst so much death and devastation—mostly people of color in sandwich board signs, handing out flyers for lunch specials and sales—made me want to cry.

The one flyer I kept for my journal was not about food, but faith. Titled "Remembrance," it featured a photo of the burning towers and people trying to outrun the massive column of gray smoke, close-ups of fire fighters and rescue workers, and some prayers from Reverend Billy Graham. Reading the passages from Psalms and Isaiah, I wondered how many of the victims of the World Trade Center attack had prayed before the flames burst into their offices.

While the exact chain reaction that caused the towers to disintegrate is as beyond my understanding as the precise chemical makeup of the lingering fumes, it's clear that the intense heat of the fires heated up the steel to a temperature that exceeded its melting point, weakening the steel columns and beams and other supports, already damaged by the impact of the airline crashes. The towers were strong enough to withstand the mechanical assaults of the two planes, but not the explosions of two tanks of jet fuel. That fire, at the time of this writing, continues to burn. "Until it runs out of fuel or until you can get to it to put water on it, it will continue to burn," said Arthur Cote, senior vice president and chief engineer with the National Fire Protection Association, in an interview on October 26, 2001.

As we watched the tendrils of smoke curl into the empty space where the towers had been, a song I didn't want to think of droned in my head—Randy Newman's sarcastic tribute to the Cuyahoga, "Burn On."

When the Cuyahoga caught fire in 1969 for the third time in the twentieth century, I thought of all the small fires I'd averted by stomping out my mother's discarded still-lit cigarettes. I was always worried back then that a candy wrapper or scrap of newspaper from the littered sidewalk would ignite, worried also when she flicked a butt beneath the greasy Rapid Transit tracks, or when the screeching train we rode to my piano lessons shot sparks at the black river beneath us. For much of the industrial twentieth century, the Cuyahoga was a dumping ground for raw sewage and chemical waste, a witch's brew where no fish, not even leeches and sludge worms survived. Subsurface gasses belched upward, past rainbow-iridescent oil pools, and when the sparks of a passing train hit the volatile petroleum derivatives one day that June, the flames leaped five stories high.

It took a while for the story to go national, but when it did, the Cuyahoga on fire became a symbol of environmental degradation, a symbol that gave momentum to the drive to pass the Clean Water Act of 1972. Now, as Cathy photographed the giant red crane digging into a pile of black rubble the same five-stories-height of the Cuyahoga fire, I wondered how we, as a nation, would ultimately turn this spectacle into a symbol: not the towers declaring America's global economic dominance, nor the airplane flying through them—that millennial nightmare we thought we'd averted—but this tall red crane itself. The thing hauling away the ruins.

I thought of the junkyard crane I always saw from the window of the West Park Rapid Transit scooping up piles and piles of crushed cars, the detritus of our then-thriving automobile industry and expanding highway system. On trips back from college, the crane signaled to me that I was back in the neighborhood. Home.

In 1969, when the Cuyahoga caught fire and when my mother started taking me on the Rapid Transit for piano lessons in Shaker, many friends of mine from school had to move because I-90 was coming, tearing down the houses on their street. It seemed then that the whole world was one big engine run on oil and gasoline; highways expanding like a runaway fire; oil oozing out of tankers, choking marine life and blackening beaches; cities torched in race riots; Vietnam villages bursting into flame by napalm, a jellied gasoline. At night I awoke sweating from apocalyptic dreams.

As time passed, and my Social Studies teacher (the only fresh-out-of-college hipster in our school) told us about pollution and its causes, I took solace in the belief that the day would come when there was no more room for new highways and cars. I was certain that the Clean Air and Water Acts, along with the 1973 Oil Embargo, would mandate that we find alternative, cleaner, renewable sources of energy. And when our own oil production began to drop in 1970, and OPEC spiked up their prices three years later, it did seem that we really could learn to curb our old hungers. Even President Jimmy Carter appeared on TV in a cardigan imploring his fellow Americans to turn down their thermostats, telling us about the solar panels he was installing in the White House and the new forty-mile-per-gallon cars we would soon be driving. But then Ronald Reagan came in, a fossil from the bigger-is-better era, with his cronies from the fossil fuel dynasties.

Now, as I stood on Church and Vesey, watching the red crane lower to pick up debris, I thought of Ronald Reagan taking down the White House solar panels, and Bush Senior allowing the Carter Executive Order for that high-mileage car to expire.

Here's what I would learn about our oil use when I got home: Since the 1982 recession, when we were using about 16 million barrels a day, to 2000, when we used about 19.5 million barrels a day, our consumption has increased about 20 percent. The most significant change is in our imports, given that our own oil production has been declining for thirty years. Imports were 6 million barrels a day in 1982, but 11 million in 2000, nearly twice the amount. Currently our nation, which contains 5 percent of the world's population, uses 25 percent of the world's oil and 43 percent of the world's gasoline. These are staggering figures, and having oil executives in the White House only means that these percentages will grow. In the 2000 election, oil and gas companies gave George W. Bush $1,889,206 in campaign funds. According to a study done by the Center for Responsive Politics, Bush "got more money from the industry during 1999-2000 than any other federal candidate over the last decade," even more than his father, which was a lot since Republicans have gotten 78 cents out of every dollar Big Oil has ever contributed to federal political parties.

But of course, Democrats are oily slicksters too. In 1979, when Carter was putting up solar panels in the White House, he was also drafting the Carter Doctrine, which states that any move by a "hostile power" to gain control of the Persian Gulf is to be regarded "as an assault on the vital interests of the United States of

America" to be resisted "by any means necessary, including military force." To this end, Carter established the Rapid Deployment Force, combat forces that, while based in the United States, were quickly available for deployment to the Persian Gulf. He also sent the U.S. warships to the Gulf, which we would ultimately use during the Gulf War under the Bush Administration. To protect the Saudi royal family, Carter also increased U.S. involvement in the kingdom's internal security operations, a relationship that Bush Senior and Bill Clinton only deepened.

And it was the Carter Administration that authorized the covert operations in the Soviet-backed regime in Afghanistan, an operation which, as Michael Klare reminded us in a November 5, 2001 article in the *Nation,* was financially fueled and fought by our friends in the Saudi regime. The kingdom allowed its citizens, including Osama bin Laden, to participate in the war effort as combatants and fund-raisers, thus arming them for future action.

Saudi Arabia is also the birthplace of fifteen of the September 11 hijackers.

No one was surprised when Bush and Cheney and the other former oil executives in the White House rejected the Kyoto Treaty, thus alienating us from much of the world, including nations we would need as allies in our war against terrorism. But regardless of our poor prospects for convincing this particular administration that we must do our part to cut down on greenhouse emissions for the sake of the ozone, there has never been a better time to make the case that our appetite for oil is a threat to our national security. Our ever-rising fuel consumption, and corresponding dependence on repressive Middle Eastern regimes, have become a liability, a weakness that, on September 11 was transformed into a weapon of mass destruction used against us.

The hijackers and the terrorist network that helped plan this genocide had symbolism in mind—our financial nerve center, our military stronghold in Washington—but I can't help but wonder if their insidious bomb of choice—jet fuel and innocent civilians—was also intended to shed light on the sycophantic relationship between the United States and the Saudi royal family. Today, over half, 56 percent, of our crude oil comes from abroad, one-sixth of it alone from Saudi Arabia.

According to Michael Klare and others, bin Laden's goal has been twofold: "the expulsion of the American 'infidels from Saudi Arabia (the heart of the Muslim Holy Land) and the overthrow of the current Saudi regime and its replacement with one more attuned to his fundamentalist Islamic beliefs." Arabian American Oil Company (ARAMCO), an alliance of major U.S. oil corporations and its U.S. partners, have reaped immense profits from their operations in Saudi Arabia and from the distribution of Saudi oil worldwide.

Profitable or not, our vital interests have cost us dearly. Rob Nixon, writing in the *New York Times* on October 29, 2001, noted that importing "oil costs the United States over $250 billion a year, if one includes federal subsidies and the health and environmental impact of air pollution. America spends $56 billion on the oil itself and another $25 billion on the military defense of oil-exporting Middle Eastern countries." Michael Klare puts the latter figure closer to $50 billion.

These are outrageously high numbers, but what's even more disturbing is that Saudi Arabia funnels money from oil earnings to extreme organizations and anti-Western terrorists and, when asked by the Bush Administration after the attacks, refused to do background checks on the hijackers from the kingdom, all of them suspected to be members of these organizations. These kickbacks are like the protection money a restaurant owner in a Mafia district gives to the Brethren just to stay in business. It's hush money to keep the dissidents of a corrupt authoritarian monarchy from taking to the streets. And apparently, American intelligence has known about this for a long time. According to an article by Seymour M. Hersh, "King's Ransom," from the October 22, 2001 *New Yorker,* National Security Agency intercepts "have demonstrated to analysts that by 1996 Saudi money was supporting Osama bin Laden's Al Qaeda and other extremist groups in Afghanistan, Lebanon, Yemen, and Central Asia, and throughout the Persian Gulf region."

The Saudi royal family has also given money and technical assistance to Hamas, the extremist Islamic group that targets Israel. The latter was brought home to me the day before our walk to the crash site, when we'd been in a taxi and a call-in radio show came on asking listeners to debate whether or not Mayor Rudolf Giuliani had done the right thing when he refused a Saudi prince's offer of $10 million. The check had come with strings attached—that we begin to rethink our policies in the Middle East. The prince (who owns a veritable Monopoly board of Manhattan's prime real estate) was referring to our backing of Israel, not his own kingdom, but what stayed with me was the Bush Administration's quickness to try to make nice with our insulted Arab "friend" in the wake of Giuliani's rejection.

Everyone knows that the royal family's conspicuous displays of wealth have alienated it from the larger Saudi population. The kingdom's $50 billion worth of oil exports accounts for 90 percent of all export receipts, 32 percent of the kingdom's GDP, and 75 percent of the government's revenues, but not much of it seems to benefit the people. Meanwhile, American-owned construction and oil companies do billions of dollars worth of business every year with the world's largest oil producer, including Halliburton, Dick Cheney's old company.

It is important to remember here that Saudi Arabia follows the same Wahhabi strain of Islam that the Afghan Taliban adheres to, which would make the U.S. presence near Mecca, let alone the U.S. presence in the culture in any form, a religious affront. And not only are we seen by devout Muslims as an economic and cultural influence of corruption but we're seen as the might—the supplier of weapons, or veritable armies—behind the throne. While an Islamic state might ban television and radio and some newspapers to shut out all news of the West, Saudi Arabia goes further than this by outlawing all forms of political debate while using its U.S.-trained security forces to squash all signs of dissent. The kingdom already has no political parties, no right of assembly, no free speech, and no opportunity to legally critique a governing family that skims off huge percentages of its oil profits for home use. "All these effects," Klare points out, "have generated covert opposition to the regime and occasional acts of violence— and it is from this underground milieu that Osama bin Laden has drawn his inspiration and many of his top lieutenants."

But even if our relationship with Saudi Arabia falters, the Middle East and Asia are sure to offer us other ways to get our fix of what Linda Hogan calls "the black blood of earth." As recently as 1999, Halliburton was planning to expand to the Caspian Sea, near the north-west of Afghanistan, which holds an estimated 6 billion barrels of oil reserves, enough, as Arundhati Roy has written scathingly in "Brutality Smeared in Peanut Butter," "to meet American energy needs for the next 30 years (or a developing country's energy requirements for a couple of centuries)." And as American airlines have cleaned house to adjust to a post–9/11 economic climate, at least one candidate for CEO has strong links to this region. A nominee for United's most senior executive used to be on the board of Unocal, another oil company that used to employ some of Bush Senior and Junior's cabinet members. As recently as the summer of 2001, Unocal was hoping to drum up some business with the Taliban.

This oil corridor through Afghanistan will most likely become one of our spoils of war.

These oh-so-American values of individuality and mobility that we are fighting to uphold are and will continue to be code words for the right to depend on cheap oil from corrupt kingdoms, on ever-expanding highway and airway systems in our nation and the nations we control, on cheap domestic labor (or will airport security finally get a living wage thanks to recent decisions in Congress?), and the virtual enslavement of millions of laborers the world over, all delivered to us by transnational media actors who are trained to say, "What the terrorists hate is our freedom."

This same freedom, of course, is what gave my friend and me the opportunity to drive for seven hours to watch rescue workers dig through a mass grave.


As Cathy took her last photograph, I whispered, "Let's get out of here right now." Only fifteen minutes had passed since we'd arrived at the barrier, but I felt that I'd been there half a century.

We hurried away to City Hall, then caught a cab to the hotel. We had plans to go to galleries with my stepson but we had to lie down until we felt well enough to do our patriotic duty by putting a nice wad of tourist money into the city coffers.


I won't go into the rest of our New York visit, how our Punjabi cab driver with his American flag sticker on the driver door was thrilled that we recognized where he and his turban hailed from, and how, by sheer fluke, we got him twice in one day, first on our way past NBC just as the NBC Anthrax case was being announced on the radio, and then on our way to buy my husband a watch. I won't go into what a pleasure it was to have lunch with Dawn in the Upper West Side café where *You've Got Mail* was featured, and to see my stepson's gorgeous paintings, then dine with him at our favorite Northern Italian café. I won't even describe how oddly comforting it was to see *Hedda Gabbler*, to savor an old-fashioned nineteenth-century melodrama (what a relic of a bygone, innocent age! how hopelessly uncomplicated this bourgeois family's conflicts seemed!) even though I wondered, when the audience gasped as Hedda, a deliciously wicked general's daughter, shot herself offstage, if such a collective response was more poignant because the tragic events of this autumn had given everyone the jitters. All I'll say is that our love and interest in this vital metropolis were renewed, but that the city's anxiety caught up to us in the end. We were, I confess, glad when it was time to go home.

The streets were emptier than usual as we left on Sunday morning, a day when New York was rumored to be a target for another terrorist attack. We both had to work the next day, so we were glad not to get stalled in traffic. We hoped we'd shave off a little of the seven hours if we stopped only once.

In Warrensburg, just off Route 87, the Gateway to the Adirondacks, we made our pit stop at a Citgo station. The roads north of Albany had been clogged with students coming back from midsemester break, and it was hard to find a space at the pump amidst all the trucks and SUVs. They were everywhere—not an economy car in sight. I had to maneuver carefully to get my Toyota Corolla in between two SUVs with American flags flapping off their hoods, and I can't begin to describe my intense feelings of anomie. That's when the lesson of the last few weeks really came home to me, and I was struck hard. I found myself remembering that one-off *West Wing* episode that came out three weeks after the attack—a pedantic series of lectures by the usually liberal and idealistic Bartlet Adminstration staffers about the hows and whys of terrorism, each lesson punctuated by a commercial for big luxury cars. "You Know You Want It," the jingle ran. "Dare to dream."

All through the sometimes-Bartlet-like Clinton years, while I was wondering why I couldn't buy a vehicle that got fifty miles to the gallon and four-wheel drive, the roads were filling up with these trucks (half of all vehicles, I've since read) and Rodeos and Navigators and Yukons and Explorers and Grand Cherokees, to say nothing of all the Range Rovers Cathy and I saw in Manhattan. Gas guzzling is obviously a bipartisan pastime, so is it any wonder that a bill introduced this fall in Congress to require higher mileage of cars and SUVS failed?

I couldn't get out of that Citgo lot fast enough.

"Do you smell something?" I said to Cathy, a few miles later.

"Are you sure you screwed on the top after you filled the tank?"

"I am," I said, and then I realized that the gasoline stink was coming from inside the car. The aroma saturated my hair and my sleeves. My headache and nausea from the day before were back, and it felt like the toxic spewage from the wreckage site had followed us, uncannily, into my car. We opened the car windows, and then, at the McDonald's in Tupper Lake, I tried in vain to scrub the smell off my hands. When I went to sleep, a faint residue of the odor still remained, as it would the next morning when, punching the key words "vital interests" into a search engine to begin my crash course on U.S. oil consumption, an ad for an SUV—a Rodeo, the biggest in its class—flashed onto my screen.

**REFERENCES CITED**

Annual Energy Review, 2000. www:ceia.doe.gov

Bachman, Danny. "Saudi Arabia versus Globalization," *theGlobalist*, September 20, 2001. www.theglobalist.com

Gonzalez, Juan. "A Toxic Nightmare at Disaster Site," *New York Daily News Online*, October 26, 2001. www.nydailynews.com

Hersh, Seymour M. "King's Ransom." *New Yorker.* October 22, 2001. info.state.gov/topical/environ/latest

Klare, Michael T. "The Geopolitics of War." *Nation.* November 5, 2001.

Nixon, Rob. "A Dangerous Appetite for Oil." *New York Times.* October 29, 2001.

Roy, Arundhati. "Brutality Smeared in Peanut Butter: Why America Must Stop the War Now." *Guardian,* October 23, 2001.

Schwartz, Alan. Professor of Environmental Studies at St. Lawrence University. Personal Interview, October 26, 2001.

"U.S. Anti-Terrorist Strategy—First Kill All the SUVs." *theGlobalist*, October 17, 2001. www.theglobalist.com

U.S. Department of State. International Information Programs. "No Health Effects from Gulf War Fires, DOD Says." September 28, 2000.

Ross Glover, *Infinite End. Reprinted with the permission of Ross Glover.*

# 14. The War on _____

Ross Glover

Fill in the blank. Regardless of what word you insert, the American public understands. U.S. presidents learned this lesson well over the last forty years. "The War on _____" plays on our competitive heartstrings like a football cheer. "Yes," we seem to respond, "fight the good fight, O fearless President, fight the war for us, fight the war for the good of humanity, but most importantly just fight." It matters little that most fights end up only wasting time, money, and lives, or that every time we begin fighting, conditions get worse rather than better. Fight anyway; fight all the way; fight to the death for the sake of freedom and democracy, or their new incarnation—homeland security. A social itch needs scratching, something seems not quite right, so we must fight it, strap on the guns, crank up the jets, arm the missiles, and fight, dammit! Fight! Could we not instead gather together to work on the problem, find solutions, and implement those solutions as an international community?

No, this is a "War on _____." We must fight, fight, fight. America is strong—we don't work together—we fight the War on _____. No namby-pamby talking, let's act now—fight now— kill now—maybe later we will think? With a war on, who has time to remember that the leader of this war was not democratically elected? With a war on, who has time to think about who's leading? We must simply fight. Our president certainly knows this, and from his father's experience, he knows that if you want high approval ratings, declare "War on _____." How fortunate for his political hopes, he now has the ultimate war to wage, a war against an ever-changing enemy, a war that permits the use of massive military force virtually indiscriminately.

Could it get any better for U.S. citizens who love to see explosions carried out in their name? The War on Terror(ism)[1] is here, and CNN's ratings are soaring. I wonder, however, if we might reflect on what it means for a U.S. president to declare war on something. In this essay, I examine three of these declarations: the War on Poverty, the War on Drugs, and the War on Terror(ism). Indoctrinated independently and at different times, all three exhibit similar characteristics.

One of the easiest things for an American president to declare a war on is an idea too vague to fight or too broad to be meaningful. The three "wars on" exemplify this reality. Poverty, drugs, and terrorism have a variety of common aspects, but as things to fight, the most important is the fact that they represent broad ideas that have little real meaning. Of the three, only drugs are actual things. Poverty and terror are social or personal states, and terrorism is so vague, the *BBC World Service* has stopped using the term altogether. We feel terror and we experience poverty. Drugs are, of course, real things, but they are so many things that the word "drugs" has very little meaning in and of itself. Some drugs are good (antibiotics), some drugs are happy (prozac, marijuana), some drugs are great (Viagra), some drugs are normal (caffeine), and other drugs are evil incarnate (heroin). Poverty, terror(ism), and drugs share the strange similarity of nonspecificity. The definition of each determines the strategy to attack them. And more often than not, the definitions change with the political will to orchestrate a new kind of war. To be sure, the invocation of "war" powerfully imposes a position against something, but it also implies an active attack. What does it mean to attack vague concepts? Answering this question may also answer the question, what is this present war on?

In the 1960s President Johnson declared a comprehensive War on Poverty. Starving Americans make for bad press, and Johnson took some serious steps to change the distribution of wealth within the country. Of course, he also started sending a large number of Americans to their deaths in Vietnam. Nevertheless, his War on Poverty did have a comprehensive welfare package as well as a focus on affirmative action policies that addressed the overall disadvantage of minority groups and women in the economic workplace. Why, however, call it a *war* on poverty? When a nation goes to war, it willingly enters into a process legitimating, requiring, and producing bloodshed. Should we understand the war on poverty as an active decision of the U.S. government to kill people in order to end poverty? If so, who gets killed? Do we kill the rich because they have money that can be dispersed to people in poverty? Or do we kill the poor, since getting rid of the poor inherently gets rid of poverty? Is this what Johnson meant by a war on poverty? Of course not, he wanted to end the conditions that caused many Americans to starve to death, commit crimes, die young, live without running water, suffer racial discrimination, and become addicted to drugs. A war on poverty has one major problem, however: fighting poverty makes no sense.

In order to eradicate poverty, we must give to others, not fight them; we must change the conditions that create poverty by changing the ways we live, think, and distribute wealth; and we must care about the impoverished. All these things run counter to war. If we must fight, should we not fight when fighting actually makes sense and would be beneficial? Poverty is a social condition in which people do not have enough. How can a war be fought against absence? How could such a war ever be sensible?

Too many people without enough, let's declare war. Maybe we should declare war on clean water; there are too many people without enough of that. Or how about a war on maternity leave or healthcare or even leisure time, way too many people without enough of these things. It could certainly make for interesting headlines—"President George W. Bush Declares War on Leisure Time." This would be a much less innocuous war than the War on Drugs declared by Richard Nixon less than a decade after Johnson's war on poverty.

Long before Nixon declared his War on Drugs, the United States actively sought the elimination of illicit drugs from its streets. At the International Opium Commission in 1909, the United States began a large-scale global insurgency against narcotics and forced most European countries to impose serious domestic policies against drugs. Each decade since has had its own drug panic and prohibition. One illicit drug or another occupies the official rhetoric as public enemy number one, and often non-illicit drugs become illicit. This history gave Nixon an excellent platform on which to launch an international war on drugs. Nixon had two clear objectives in his war on drugs, and along with these objectives came two clear ironies. Nixon's proposed war focused on (1) the elimination of addiction in the United States (and to his credit, Nixon funded treatment proportionately more than any other president since); and (2) the elimination of suppliers of illicit drugs, that is, a focus on international drug trafficking. Ironically, the plan's focus on treatment emerged because a large percentage of U.S. troops returned home from Vietnam addicted to heroin. Equally ironic, the plan needed to focus on supply because the CIA had been actively supporting opium growers in Southeast Asia since the late 1940s, as well as suppliers in South Vietnam. This manifestation of the War on Drugs showed promising signs, with an initial reduction in drug use, crime, and manufacturing. Unfortunately, the international political involvement of the CIA and the Drug Enforcement Agency as well as the progressive erosion of the treatment budget for the war on drugs led to a strengthening of the drug trafficking circuits out of Asia and the Middle East. When Soviet forces invaded Afghanistan in 1979, the country was only a minor player in the global drug trade. In our efforts to support the *mujahideen* (the Islamic resistance fighters, including Osama bin Laden, and others whom Ronald Reagan called "freedom fighters"), the DEA and the CIA watched silently and supportively as the Pakistan-Afghan area captured more than 60 percent of the global heroin market. This is a war on drugs? Allow a greater supply of heroin abroad while reducing treatment programs at home and increasing prison sentences for drug offenses? We have been fighting a war on drugs and that war has been against American citizens. We fund our covert operations and other countries' military actions by the active involvement in or the passive permitting of drug trafficking.

While using the vague and often unspecified term "drugs" after the phrase "the War on," U.S. foreign policy makers potentially justify any global military activity. However, the frightening reality is that the war on drugs has had much more to do with promoting U.S. business interests than with any drug. In the name of democracy, the Reagan-Bush Administration actively used drug trafficking to fund a rebel army in Nicaragua. These so-called Contras, groups often trained by the CIA, and also called "Freedom Fighters" by President Reagan, murdered supporters of socialist democratic ideals. These ideals sought an end to poverty and a beginning to national education and healthcare for all citizens, not to mention a stable economy. Reagan, while producing the most fervent fear and the most viciously articulated war on drugs, was simultaneously supporting and funding the narcotics trade in Central America; these drugs, primarily cocaine, were destined for the U.S. market. Not simply carrying out blind-eye policies, the CIA, Oliver North, Vice President Bush, and numerous others actively supported, paid for, and traded with those trafficking in narcotics, ostensibly to pay for the overthrow of governments concerned with their citizens' poverty and to support some of the harshest dictatorial regimes in the Americas. These activities took place under the rubric of a "war on drugs."

As they actively traded in illegal narcotics and illegal weapons, the Reagan Administration created the term "narcoterrorism" to describe the people in Central America we were supposedly fighting against. The use of this term attempted to justify any and all military action in the region. So the war on drugs, a vague thing at best, became a war against narcoterrorists. In Reagan's words, "The link between the governments of such Soviet allies as Cuba and Nicaragua and international narcotics trafficking and terrorism is becoming increasingly clear. The twin evils—narcotics trafficking and terrorism—represent the most insidious and dangerous threats to the hemisphere today."[2] The war on drugs was then a war against narcoterrorists and the relationship between Soviet allies, narcotics, and terrorism. However, we know that the opposition against Soviet forces in Afghanistan at this point represented one of the largest exporters of heroin in the world. In reality, the United States and its allies were the narcoterrorists. We only need to look at the School of the Americas to discover that the U.S. military trained foreign groups to use terrorizing tactics for the purpose of undermining governments and/or people concerned with eradicating poverty in Central America. The funding for the Contras came from nothing other than narcotics sales actively and passively supported by the United States. Many of the weapons used by Oliver North's operation came from the Middle East with $1.5 million dollars worth of weapons coming from a Syrian arms and drugs dealer named Manzer al-Kassar, a suspected terrorist in his own right.[3]

Clearly the term "narcoterrorists" acted as excellent propaganda, but the reality speaks to the fact that the United States is the biggest narcoterrorist of all. Again, the war on drugs is a war on ourselves; in this case, a legitimate fight against drug trafficking would have the U.S. government attacking its own officials. Instead, the Reagan and Bush administrations, along with Congress, destroyed the drug treatment budget and systematically increased mandatory minimum sentences for drug offenders. And in the decade of cocaine panic, crack becomes the most heavily prosecuted drug, eliciting some of the most severe prison sentences. Many critics have pointed out that the stiff sentences on crack cocaine versus the relatively mild sentences for powder cocaine underscore both racial and class biases within the legal system. Just as in Central America, the U.S. government supports domestic policies most likely to punish people in poverty. As Reagan and Bush used ideology to legitimate a war on drugs, the war they actually practiced was on the impoverished.

The primary reason that a war on drugs operates with impunity and contradiction is that a war on drugs does not mean anything. "War on" simply elicits a panicked response from the media and subsequently the population. It has no inherent meaning as such, especially when connected to terms like poverty, drugs, leisure time, or terrorism. The war on drugs acts as a noble lie through which law enforcement and the military justify active invasions into innocent people's lives. As with the war on drugs, we now see President George W. Bush using the phrase "war on" to continue the presidential legacy of using vague ideas to constrict freedoms, to increase poverty, and to permit unilateral U.S. military decisions (veiled as an international coalition) to wreak havoc across the planet. A war on terrorism produces the same old conditions upon which the war on terrorism began.

Examining the historical facts of the war on drugs, the war on terrorism (sometimes called a war on terror and other times a war against people who hate freedom)[4] is nothing other than the manifestation of the war on drugs in different form. Starting at what might be the most telling year in this history, 1967 shows two interesting things. First, it was the year that the CIA put Manuel Noriega on its payroll, and second, in that same year, Israel began its occupation of the West Bank and Gaza in direct violation of international law. While these two events occurred independently, in the years to follow Israel became a key player in the laundering of drug money and the supplying of weapons to and for Noriega and the CIA. Israel and Israeli operatives actively supported Noriega and the Contras alongside the United States as well as helped launder the money used to fund the terrorist operations against the people in Central America.

At this point in time, the importance of Israel must not be underestimated. Whether from the Right or Left, political leaders recognize the Palestine-Israel issue as a key factor to understanding the war on terrorism. The links between Israel and the war on drugs illustrate the continued state-sponsored practices that have produced the conditions we now fear. According to Eqbal Ahmad, Israeli occupation of Palestinian land generated the condition under which the PLO created modern forms of terrorism, particularly the airplane hijacking.[5] A similar phenomenon exists in the repressive Central American regimes that create the conditions under which leftist movements use guerilla tactics, labeled terrorist by U.S. politicians only when used in the service of people's well-being, to overthrow brutal governments. The creation of so-called terrorists does not occur in a vacuum, and both the United States and Israel bear the brunt of the responsibility for creating terrorizing conditions in Central America as well as in Palestine-Israel.

In the 1970s the CIA, with George Bush as its head, paid Noriega for the information he could share with them, and in so doing created one of the biggest drugs and arms smugglers in Central America. In addition, after the Carter Administration, the Reagan-Bush Administration put Noriega back on the CIA payroll, increasing his salary by 1986 to $200,000. After creating him as a major military and political leader in Panama, the Bush Administration overthrew Noriega's government and kidnapped him from his own country, and in the process destroyed the homes, entire neighborhoods at a time, of the poorest people living in Panama City. All this, from putting Noriega on the payroll to his overthrow and kidnapping to the destruction of the most impoverished people's homes, was justified in the name of the war on drugs.

The story of Noriega is not unlike the story of the Taliban. After the Soviet invasion of Afghanistan, the United States worked hard to support the *mujahideen's* resistance to Soviet forces. In support of these forces, as well as other forces across the globe, the CIA used what should be considered a postcolonial strategic alliance with narcotics trafficking to develop and maintain control. The U.S. government realized that one of the most effective ways to arm its imperial foot soldiers, whether those soldiers are Afghan, Iraqi, or Nicaraguan, is to use the drug trade to buy weapons. By assisting the heroin trade in the Afghanistan-Pakistan region, the CIA was able to fund silently and less expensively the arming and training of the resistance to the Soviet invasion. This, of course, was in addition to the $3 billion in aid given to the *mujahideen* "freedom fighters."

Clearly the other so-called war involved in these places is the Cold War, and the use of Cold War rhetoric continued to permit the types of activities the United States used throughout the 1980s. Nevertheless, the Cold War ended and the war on drugs continued, even after Drug Czar Barry McCaffrey argued that to call the war on drugs a war was to misrecognize the reality of the situation. The reality, suggested McCaffrey, before being strong-armed into following popular rhetoric, is a need for demand-side projects, that is, treatment. Yet the budget reflects steady increases in funding to law enforcement agencies rather than treatment programs.

In 2001, the George W. Bush Administration gave $43 million to the Taliban to reduce heroin production in Afghanistan. Now we have declared the Taliban enemy number two, after Osama bin Laden. We have declared a war on terrorism. Five things link the present war on terrorism and the war on drugs. First, as mentioned above, is the vagueness of the terms, drugs and terrorism. Second, the United States has supported many so-called terrorist organizations in the past in order to further its political interests (the global domination of capitalism), as it has done with drug traffickers. Third, the same regions the United States exploits for terrorist purposes seem to be those where drug trafficking gains the strongest foothold. Fourth, both "wars on" create conditions that allow law enforcement more power to enter into citizens' lives without just cause. Finally, the war on terrorism seems to attack the same types of people that the war on drugs does, the impoverished.

Since September 11, Robert Fisk, writing for the *Independent*, consistently argues that what the United States calls "terrorism" at this point has little to do with the general activities of any individuals, and everything to do with mobilizing global support for its otherwise unilateral decisions. The United States supports a variety of groups using terrorist-like tactics. During both the Bush and Clinton administrations, the CIA and U.S. political leaders actively covered up the disappearance of Efraín Bámaca Velásquez in Guatemala, even after his wife, a U.S. citizen and Harvard Law graduate, went on hunger strike in both countries demanding information about her husband. The Guatemalan government actively "disappeared" (the capture, torture, murder, and subsequent disavowal of such capture of Guatemalan citizens) thousands of people, creating not only terror among citizens, but also severe emotional trauma to those whose family members disappeared. These tactics were popular state-based terrorist tactics of Central and South American governments, particularly in the governments the United States supported.

Assuming that one could justify state-sanctioned terrorism, it should be noted that the United States also actively financed and supported less internationally legitimate acts of terrorism. Take, for example, the bombing at La Penca, Costa Rica, in which former CIA-sponsored Contra leader Edén Pastora was holding a press conference. This bombing killed two journalists and was carried out by Contras close to the CIA, according to a Costa Rican investigation. Manzar al-Kassar, the Syrian arms dealer, paid $1.5 million by Oliver North's Contra operation, is now credited with the downing of Pan Am flight 103 in 1987. And let us not forget the primary evildoer of 1990, Saddam Hussein, a national leader whose entire military infrastructure the United States helped create. While we may refer to a specific terrorist as our target in the war on terrorism, the fact remains that the United States supports as many terrorists as it fights, just as it supports many drug trafficking organizations.

Returning to Reagan's statement suggesting that narcotics trafficking and drugs represent primary evils, a statement we could certainly imagine resurfacing in the aftermath of 9/11, it seems clear that the two intertwine in the most interesting ways. As noted above, the primary export of Afghanistan and Pakistan for the last thirty years has been opium. This crop received active support from the CIA throughout that time period. At this point, of course, heroin from Afghanistan has become a serious problem, as has the Taliban, a government which actually reduced opium production. Other *mujahideen* factions, including

al-Qaeda members, benefited significantly from opium production, especially the Northern Alliance, a group in the region we
now seem to support. Given our history, should we not suspect
that the newly formed military dictatorship in Pakistan now benefits from the production of opium in that country? Should we
not also suspect that the Northern Alliance is now reaping the re-
wards of opium trafficking in the region? Almost certainly, these
things are happening as you read these words.

The United States supports narcotics trafficking at any point
in time when such trafficking funds U.S. interests. Unfortunately,
this practice also creates more problems than it solves. In almost
every country in which the United States intervenes (whether it
be to offer military support, help that country's drug trafficking
operation, or fight against a legitimate government of the people) and then withdraws after its tactical success (or even if it stays
around for that matter), the people within that country suffer
more than prior to U.S. intervention. Examples of this are too
numerous to list, but a short list would include Afghanistan, Iraq,
Colombia, Peru, El Salvador, Nicaragua, Panama, and Vietnam.

The problems created by declaring "war on _____," while
often international, also exist domestically. In fact, the domestic
effects of the war on drugs and the war on terrorism make the
two distinguishable in name only. In the Anti-Drug Abuse Act of
1986, the United States legitimated, among other things, the
seizure of anyone's assets proven to be connected with illicit
drugs. The effects of this Act have created numerous state drug
task forces that seize assets with impunity. Due to the structure of
this Act, seizures operate at the civil level and not at the criminal
level, thus forcing victims of such seizures to prove their innocence in order to reacquire their property. This translates into
state institutions actively seeking out "supposed" criminals from
whom to seize assets. Whether or not the individual is found
guilty in a criminal court, his assets remain under state control

until he can prove that the assets were not acquired through the sale and/or distribution of drugs. To clarify the implications of this practice, drug task forces have the right to confiscate the property of any U.S. citizen, and in order to reclaim their property, citizens must prove in a civil court exactly how they acquired that property. The same practices now emerge as a strategy for the war on terrorism, this time on an international scale. Anyone suspected of funding terrorists, holding the funds of terrorist organizations, or permitting the funding of terrorist organizations can have their assets frozen. This has not and does not require definitive proof. Suspicion is enough to have your assets frozen. And regardless of what we might want to believe, anyone is a potential terrorist, just as anyone is a potential drug dealer.

In addition, the law enforcement policies regarding wiretapping, surveillance, and search warrants loosened for the sake of the war on drugs have now been loosened even further in the name of the war on terrorism. In October 2001, the PATRIOT Act became law, allowing for increased wiretapping for suspected terrorists, a suspicion that will surely extend to suspected drug criminals. Certainly we have no way of knowing the ultimate effects of this Act, but it may, through its application, produce some of the most horrendous losses of civil liberties since McCarthyism. This will have been achieved in the name of a war on something that has no consistent definition, something that the United States supports as often as not.

One effect of antiterrorist legislation that is certain, however, is racism. The war on drugs created an unprecedented rise in the number of African American men in prison. The domestic side of the war on drugs produced a social system that scapegoats black male drug users to prove its effectiveness. While white people use the most drugs and receive the lowest sentences for their drug use, black men find themselves imprisoned the most and sentenced the longest. The war on crack made certain that the least expensive form of cocaine received the most prison time. The war on terrorism already functions as a racist "war on." Clearly we are not looking for white terrorists when we speak of the war on terrorism. If this were the case, the recent rash of Americans viciously attacking and sometimes killing people who look like they might be from the Middle East would not have occurred. In addition, the State Department would seek out those racists as terrorists.

The war on terrorism is war against people from the Middle East. And without question, the effects of the antiterrorism bill will generate significantly racist practices by law enforcement. Just as the war on drugs produced a racial scapegoat, so too does the war on terrorism. This might be one of the greatest dilemmas in declaring a war on _____: in order to legitimate a war on anything, an enemy must exist, and since drugs and terrorism are not themselves enemies, the American tradition is to make your enemy out of the racial Other. Which brings us to the most insidious connection between the war on drugs and the war on terrorism, namely, poverty.

News stories about Osama bin Laden's great wealth abound. The reality, however, is that so-called terrorist organizations, at least those not sponsored by the United States, tend to emerge in areas of abject poverty; this is certainly the case for Central America and the Middle East. Drugs, at least the sale and production of many illicit drugs, also emerge in areas of poverty. One reason for this is obvious. In a political and economic environment in which one has no power or wealth nor access to the possibility for such things, the informal economy and guerilla tactics produce results. Peru's largest cash crop is coca. Do farmers grow coca because they want to traffic in narcotics? No, they grow coca because it is a crop that helps them subsist. Did Palestinians start using suicide bombings because they like blowing themselves up? No, they did so because there was no other military alternative to Israel's dominant force.

While there are many other reasons for such actions, one of the basic realities is that poverty often demands extreme measures. And in a world social system in which the wealthy act with impunity and the impoverished are treated with disregard, often the only impoverished voices heard are those that find ways to make the loudest, most extreme noise. The United States constantly disregards the demands of impoverished countries, enforces its will on people with less ability to fight that will, and brutalizes the impoverished both at home and abroad. Johnson's war on poverty is real and it has been operationalized through the war on drugs and the newly articulated war on terrorism, not for the sake of ending poverty, but only to punish those who have the least. Do not forget that Afghanistan is one of the most impoverished countries in the world. The average life expectancy in the country is forty-six years, a number certain to creep lower after we finish demolishing the country's infrastructure. And let us not forget that as we claimed to wage war on Saddam Hussein, we murdered at least one hundred thousand Iraqi citizens, and our embargo led to over a million deaths from starvation. Yet, after Afghanistan, numerous political pundits claim, Iraq is next.

So war on, America, but as you do, as you hear the phrase "War on _____," know that the war is one that we cannot win. Know that the war is a war that sacrifices the disenfranchised for political ends that are dubious at best. And know (without hesitation) that the average American citizen suffers the consequences of every "war on." We will suffer when we are unjustly imprisoned; we will suffer when our friend of Arab or Persian or African descent disappears into the correctional system; we will suffer when our property is seized; we will suffer when the international hatred for the United States and its global bullying grows so large that a war on _____ becomes a World War. War on _____ is a dangerous game to play, and as informed citizens, it is time for us to recognize that these wars on _____ are nothing but a sham, a chimera designed to redirect our political focus. The war on

_____ is a war against the dispossessed, a war against nonwhite races, a war on poverty of the worst kind, killing the impoverished to support our own wealth.

## NOTES

1. The phrase "War on Terrorism" has not been standardized in the media or political rhetoric. Its usage varies between the War on Terrorism and the War on Terror. My use of "terror(ism)" is meant to reflect that discrepancy.

2. Quoted in Peter Dale Scott and Johnathan Marshall, *Cocaine Politics* (Berkeley: University of California Press, 1998).

3. Reports on al-Kassar appeared in *Newsday*, July 11, 1987, and *Los Angeles Times*, July 17, 1987.

4. The same people who supposedly hated freedom in the 1980s were self-proclaimed "friends of freedom." The same people, the *mujahideen*, Reagan called "Freedom Fighters."

5. Eqbal Ahmad, "Terrorism: Theirs and Ours," lecture given at the University of Colorado at Boulder, October 12, 1998 (http://www.sangam.org/ANALYSIS/Ahmad.htm).

## SUGGESTIONS FOR FURTHER READING

Draper, Theodore. *A Very Thin Line: The Iran-Contra Affairs.* New York: Hill and Wang, 1991.

Massing, Michael. *The Fix.* Berkeley: University of California Press, 2000.

McCoy, Alfred W. *The Politics of Heroin: CIA Complicity in the Global Drug Trade.* New York: Lawrence Hill Books, 1991.

Reeves, Jimmie L., and Richard Campbell. *Cracked Coverage: Television News, the Anti-Cocaine Crusade, and the Reagan Legacy.* Durham: Duke University Press, 1994.

# Appendix

## Alternatives to the Mainstream U.S. Media

AlterNet (http://www.alternet.org/)
Amnesty International (http://www.amnesty.org/)
Common Dreams News Center (http://www.commondreams
    .org/)
Food First (http://www.foodfirst.org/)
FreeSpeech Television (www.freespeech.org)
Global Exchange (http://www.globalexchange.org/)
Guardian Unlimited (http://www.guardian.co.uk/)
Human Rights Watch (http://www.hrw.org/)
The Independent (http://www.independent.co.uk/)
Independent Media Center (http://www.indymedia.org/)
The MediaChannel (http://www.mediachannel.org/)
Media Workers against War (http://www.mwaw.org)
Media Working Group (http://www.mwg.org/)
Middle East International (http://meionline.com/)
Middle East Research and Information Project (http://www
    .merip.org)
Mother Jones (http://www.motherjones.com/)
The Nation (http://www.thenation.com)
Posters for Peace (http://www.postersforpeace.org/)
The Progressive (http://www.theprogressive.org/)
Re:constructions (http://web.mit.edu/cms/reconstructions/)
United for a Fair Economy (http://www.ufenet.org/)
War & Peace (http://www.warpeace.org/)
Z Magazine (http://www.zmag.org/ZNET.htm)

# Contributors

KENNETH CHURCH is Assistant Professor of History at St. Lawrence University. He received his Ph.D. in History from the University of Michigan.

JOHN COLLINS is Assistant Professor of Global Studies at St. Lawrence University. He received his M.A. and Ph.D. in Comparative Studies in Discourse and Society at the University of Minnesota, where he was a MacArthur Scholar. His ongoing research is on the intersections of generation, nationalism, and memory in contemporary Palestine. He teaches courses on globalization, cultural studies, nationalism, the Middle East, and critical news media analysis.

GRANT H. CORNWELL is Professor and Chair, Department of Philosophy, St. Lawrence University. He received his M.A. and Ph.D. in philosophy from the University of Chicago, with a dissertation on Aristotelian virtue theory and the problem of cultural relativism. In his scholarly writing Cornwell explores epistemological issues within postcolonial studies, cultural studies, and critical pedagogy. In 1997 he published, with Richard Guarasci, *Democratic Education in an Age of Difference* (Jossey-Bass). In 2000, he coauthored a monograph with Eve Stoddard called

*Globalizing Knowledge: Connecting International and Intercultural Studies*, published by the Association of American Colleges and Universities (AAC&U), and most recently Cornwell and Stoddard have edited a volume of essays, *Global Multiculturalism: Comparative Perspectives on Ethnicity, Race, and Nation* (Rowman and Littlefield, 2000). They are currently doing research for a book on the semiotics of sugar mill ruins in the Caribbean. Cornwell is on the advisory board for AAC&U's recent initiative "Liberal Education and Global Citizenship: The Arts of Democracy," and is a fellow in the "National Learning Communities" project sponsored by the Washington Center for Improving the Quality of Undergraduate Education. At St. Lawrence, Cornwell is a member of the Caribbean and Latin American Studies program, coordinates the study abroad program in Trinidad, and serves on the advisory board for the new major in Global Studies. He teaches courses in ethical and political theory, Africana philosophy, and comparative studies of race and ethnicity.

R. DANIELLE EGAN, Ph.D., is an Assistant Professor of Sociology at St. Lawrence University, where she teaches courses in sexuality, the body, social theory, qualitative methodology, deviance, and social control. Her research on exotic dancers and their regular customers draws on poststructural theory, psychoanalysis, cultural geography, and feminist theory. She is currently working on a manuscript entitled *The Phallus Palace: Sexy Spaces, Desiring Subjects and the Fantasy of Objects* and an anthology entitled *Flesh for Fantasy: The Culture of Exotic Dance.*

ROSS GLOVER is Visiting Professor of Sociology at St. Lawrence University. His current research on encoding explores the relationship of representation and technology to the construction of human subjectivity. His publications include "French Kissing with Jurgen Habermas" in *Social Moments*, "I Only Speak One

Language: It Is Derrida's" in *Jouvert*, and "A(u) Pair a(u) Princess" in the *Canadian Journal of Social and Political Thought*. He has been Assistant Editor of *Humanity and Society* and Managing Editor of *Social Moments: A Journal of Possibilities and Positions*.

MARINA A. LLORENTE is Assistant Professor of Spanish Language and Peninsular Literature in the Department of Modern Languages and Literatures at St. Lawrence University. She earned her Ph.D. in Spanish at the University of Kansas in 1997 and is the author of *Palabra y deseo: Espacios transgresores en la poesia española, 1975–1990* (*Word and Desire: Transgressive Spaces in Contemporary Spanish Poetry, 1975–1990*), as well as articles on the emerging generation of social poets in contemporary Spain. Her research interests also include gender and cultural studies.

ERIN MCCARTHY currently teaches Asian and comparative philosophy at St. Lawrence University as a Visiting Assistant Professor. Recent publications include "The Knowing Body," in *Sagesse du corps* (Éditions du Scribe, 2001); "Le corps dans la philosophie japonaise contemporaine," in *Corps et Science: Enjeux culturels et philosophiques* (Liber, 1999); and "Teaching Comparative Philosophy: Reflections," forthcoming, in the *ASIANetwork Exchange, A Newsletter for Teaching about Asia* (winter 2001). Her current research focuses on the resonance between contemporary Japanese philosophy and Western feminist philosophies of ethics and the body.

PHILIP T. NEISSER, Associate Professor in the Department of Politics at SUNY Potsdam, earned a Masters degree at Georgetown University and received his Ph.D. from the University of Massachusetts at Amherst in 1990. Winner of a SUNY Potsdam 2000 Presidential Award for Excellence in Teaching, Neisser is primarily trained in political theory, but has since branched out into the study of social welfare policy, trade policy, and issues posed by globalization. In general, his work focuses on the ways power is shaped by prevailing narratives, whether these narratives are about the importance of family, the nature of poor people, the nature of government, or the power of the global economy. Most recently, he coedited *Tales of the State: Narrative in Contemporary U.S. Politics and Public Policy* (Rowman and Littlefield, 1997).

LAURA J. REDIEHS is Assistant Professor of Philosophy at St. Lawrence University. She is interested in the problem of the incommensurability of paradigms or worldviews, both as a problem studied within philosophy of science, and as a problem addressed by theories of nonviolent conflict resolution. In particular, she is interested in how social-constructivist theories of knowledge can help address this problem: how language use and the concept formation of social groups can serve to reinforce or dissolve apparent incommensurability across different worldviews or conceptual schemes.

LEAH RENOLD, Visiting Assistant Professor in Religious Studies at St. Lawrence University, received her Ph.D. in the history of modern South Asia and her M.A. in Asian Studies, both from the University of Texas at Austin. Her research is on modern developments within Hinduism, particularly the rise of Hindu nationalism in the last century.

NATALIA RACHEL SINGER is an Associate Professor of English at St. Lawrence University, and a contributing editor to the *North American Review*. Her essays and short stories have been published in many magazines and journals, including *Ms., Harper's, American Scholar, Creative Nonfiction, Shenandoah, Iowa Review, Prairie Schooner,* and *O.* She is also the editor, with Neal Burdick, of an anthology of creative nonfiction, *Living North Country: Essays on Life and Landscapes in Northern New York.*

EVE WALSH STODDARD is Chair of the Global Studies Department and Professor of English at St. Lawrence University. Her Ph.D. is from the University of California at Los Angeles. Having studied the history and literary representations of slavery in eighteenth- and nineteenth-century Britain, she is currently working in Caribbean cultural studies. She has co-edited, with Grant Cornwell, a book called *Global Multiculturalism: Comparative Perspectives on Ethnicity, Race, and Nation* (Rowman and Littlefield, 2000), and they are writing a book on the semiotics of sugar mill ruins as postcolonial icons of national history and identity.

PATRICIA M. THORNTON is an Assistant Professor in the Department of Political Science at Trinity College in Hartford, Connecticut. She earned her Ph.D. in Political Science from the University of California at Berkeley in 1997, and received a postdoctoral research fellowship from the Fairbank Center for East Asian Research at Harvard University the following year. Her research interests include Chinese rural politics, popular protest, social movements, political corruption, and the role of language in mobilizing collective action.

THOMAS F. THORNTON joined the Department of Global Studies at St. Lawrence University in 2001 after a decade in Juneau, Alaska, where he taught at the University of Alaska, worked as a resource specialist for the Alaska Department of Fish and Game, and conducted a wide range of field research. His Ph.D. is in sociocultural anthropology and his research interests are primarily in Native North America, especially among the Native peoples of Alaska and Canada; he has also lived and worked in mainland China and Taiwan. Currently, he has two broad areas of interest:

one is subsistence economies (particularly among indigenous peoples) and their relationship to capitalist economies at the local, national, and global levels; the other is in the human sense of place and its many cultural dimensions and reconfigurations in a rapidly changing and increasingly interconnected "global village." In addition, he does collaborative work with tribes and other Native entities on cultural and natural resource management issues affecting their sacred places and subsistence lifeways.

ANDREW D. VAN ALSTYNE has taught sociology at St. Lawrence University and is a graduate student in sociology at the University of Michigan. His interests are in political economy, environmental sociology, globalization and development, historical sociology, and social movements.

ZONE 4 is an informal collective of artists who make books and digital photography. The works submitted for *Collateral Language* were created by Ted C. Ford and Carole Mathey.